Agitato

AGITATO

A Trek through the Musical Jungle

JEROME TOOBIN

The Viking Press / New York

Acknowledgment is made to New Directions Publishing Corp., J. M.
Dent & Sons Ltd., and the Trustees for the Copyrights of the late Dylan
Thomas for quotation from "Lament" from *The Poems of Dylan
Thomas.* Copyright 1952 by Dylan Thomas. Reprinted by permission.

To Marlene

Agitato

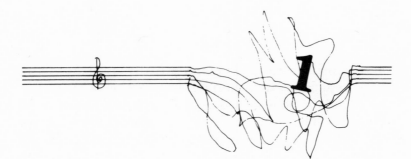

I don't go to musical events much any more. In fact, a recent visit to a Philadelphia Orchestra concert was my first in New York in many years—maybe ten. I just didn't want to be around the players and the audience and the halls. Carnegie Hall, Lincoln Center, Town Hall, Hunter Auditorium—all had their memories—and they were almost all bad. And yet, they had once been my El Dorado, my ultima Thule—you name the place where all the dreams come true, and one lives happily ever after in the world of music. Music was the great unrequited love of my life, and I suppose, we were like Spinoza and God; just because I loved it, it didn't have to love me back. But it certainly gave me a very hard time. A very hard time.

This is not essentially an autobiographical work. I have no illusions about my interest to the reader as compared with that of my *dramatis personae*. But I must give some facts as to how I got involved in the music business, and particularly as to how I got to the helm of the creaky vessel which the NBC Symphony became in its Symphony of the Air period—the post-Toscanini era.

As a boy in Philadelphia I studied the violin from my eighth year. At thirteen I was good enough to be accepted as a pupil of the estimable Mme. Lea Luboshutz at the Curtis Institute. But I never really loved the violin, and the aspiring musician not only must love his art but must indeed be obsessed by it. The young Boston conductor Michael Tilson Thomas, when asked how a young musician knew if he had the real call, said that if he could spend a single day away from his music without palpable suffering, he wasn't cut out for the profession. I had no such dedication to the fiddle. For one thing, the violin is an excruciatingly difficult instrument to master, and short of the genius (and even with it) of a Heifetz or an Oistrakh, requires a grueling regimen. Besides, I had other transcending musical interests. I suffered, of course, from that exotic Philadelphia affliction—Stokowskiitis. A symptom of that ailment is hallucinations about being a conductor. So I studied music in general, but neglected the violin.

In my early teens I studied harmony, theory, and the rudiments of conducting with William Happich, a nasty old martinet scarcely known outside of Philadelphia. There were vague rumors that he had had some contact with Mahler as a youth, but he was far too unpleasant and aloof for anyone to ask him about it.

I also played violin and viola in the Symphony Club Orchestra, a local training group organized by Mr. Happich. I remember my first rehearsal there all too well. The piece was Beethoven's *Prometheus* Overture, tricky at the outset for the strings. I distinguished myself at one point by playing all by myself, while the other strings rested. Alas, Beethoven was with them, not me. Happich glared murderously at me—all thirteen years of me—and shuddered.

"Nitwit!" he barked out at the hapless fiddle player

trying to hide under his chair. "Ach, such a nitwit," he added, reassuringly.

I studied orchestral scores assiduously. And this caused great friction between my father and me. Joseph S. Toobin, a pharmacist by trade, was a self-proclaimed expert on all pedagogical matters, but he was especially expert, it seemed, in music. After all, he turned on the New York Philharmonic every Sunday. True, he dozed off after five or six minutes, but he was a hard-working druggist whose hours were like those of a worker in the jute mills of the nineteenth century. (Actually, falling asleep to music is a sweetly sensuous sensation, and I've done it myself lots of times.) J. S. Toobin declared definitively that all conductors had to be instrumental virtuosi first. He scoffed at my conducting aspirations. My indifference to the violin, he asserted, made my conductorial ambitions quixotic at best. So we fought. I was an early advocate of Shaw's theories on the "myth of parental wisdom."

Thus my father, quite literally by force, kept me in the public-school system, and out of a full music curriculum at Curtis. Only the baffling constancy of Mme. Luboshutz kept me in Curtis at all. But soon my father's disapproval of my musical plans brought him to the office of Josef Hoffman, then the director of Curtis. My father assured me, and I'm sure he was telling the truth, that he read Hoffman a stern lecture on how to run a music school. Not long after that golden moment for the great pianist, I was severed from all connections with the Curtis Institute. It managed quite nicely without me.

I was then fourteen. My father, who was considerably older, continued to sneer at any idea I had for a conducting future. He insisted that if I applied myself, the violin would make me rich and famous. Actually, there was no chance in the world that it would make me either. I was studying the violin privately now with Jascha Simkin, a first violinist in the Philadelphia Orchestra for many years, and a good teacher. Thinking of Jascha Simkin and those stormy days with papa, who seemed obsessed with the glories of the fiddle, brings to mind the odd tale of how I was named—or was it misnamed?

I appeared on the scene in the Jefferson Hospital, a Philadelphia landmark, on December 6, 1922. Through some traditional Hebrew system I was to be named for my great-grandfather Jacob, but my father had other ideas. Joseph S. Toobin, believing I assume in associational glory, registered me with the Bureau of Vital Statistics as Jascha (no middle name) Toobin. I was named after Jascha Heifetz, who then only twenty-one was already a legend, especially in the Jewish communities. J. S. Toobin, however, neglected to tell his wife, my mother, the former Tillie Gudelman, of this naming until I was a day old. How this came about was never clear, since most parents usually reason together on what their offspring will be called, often years before said offspring spring off. But J. S. Toobin wasn't much of a consulter, and somehow he never got around to telling my mother until the second day. Here Tillie Gudelman Toobin, generally passive, the perfect mate for the non-consulting J. S. Toobin, turned quite violent, if I am to credit her account. "Over my dead body you'll call him Jascha. Jascha? Would you like to play with the other kids with a name like Jascha? Never. My son won't walk down the street with the kids yelling, 'Hey, Yash!' Never."

Well, after all these years I'm a little baffled at this uncharacteristic outburst. And I must admit that I don't think "Hey, Yash" would have turned me to stone—or ablaze with embarrassment. True, I can't picture an outfielder for the Yankees (one of my favorite daydream occupations) called Jascha or, for that matter, to speak of a humbler position, a U.S. senator from Pennsylvania. But no matter, I had very little to do with it, and the name was anathema to Tillie. Papa, frightened I suppose by the passions Tillie evinced in what he took to be her delicate postnatal state (she later told me she never felt better in her life) relented, and Jascha, as a name, died aborning. Now they did reason together, and Tillie, still for some reason deeply concerned with my future outdoor activity, also rejected the traditional Jacob, because she didn't want people yelling, "Hey, Jake," when they wanted or needed her pride and joy. I'm astonished that my quite timid and reticent mother seemed from birth to see me perpetually at the beck and call of multitudes.

J. S. T: So what can we call him?

TILLIE: Jerome sounds nice. How about Jerome?

J. S. T: O.K., Jerome. Now rest, I didn't think it would be such a big thing. You know what Jascha Heifetz made just from records last year?

TILLIE: Joe, I'm tired. I think I'll take a nap.

And so, Jerome.

Having skipped a year in grade school, I was ready to graduate from high school at sixteen. This led to my last hurrah as a would-be conductor. My intrepid father was now arranging for me to get a scholarship to Temple University, his alma mater. I balked. I told him I wanted to reapply to Curtis as a conducting student. He said this was "idiotic," one of his favorite terms where my doings were concerned. "Learn to play the violin first. Then we'll see." Whatever that meant. When I got adamant, he said, "You want to be a lunatic, O.K. But not a damn thing do I give you for anything. You want to be a conductor, get the hell out and support yourself." (Probably the best advice he ever gave me in my life.) He would always give me the same sneer when he said "conductor," as though it were a euphemism for pimp or numbers-runner. And he would wax funny. "Yeah, you'll be a conductor. On the 'Seventy' you'll be a conductor." The "Seventy" was the trolley car connecting my neighborhood and the center of Philadelphia.

Well, I can belabor Joseph S. Toobin, and he deserves some belaboring, as do all us mortals. In the last analysis, I'm certain that if I had really had the call or the need or whatever it is that hurdles the obstacles and gets to the goal, I would have sent J. S. Toobin to hell, told him to shove Temple, and become a conductor. After all, I hear tell that old man Toscanini thought that Arturo's musical career would wind up with him playing the cello in a whorehouse. The Toscanini family didn't even come to the first concert that Arturo conducted in Parma, his hometown. But some comparisons are really odious—and the Toscanini-Toobin one is, to quote my father, "idiotic." Either I didn't have the call or the talent or the guts—probably all three—because I buckled and went to Temple, and I never even became a conductor on the "Seventy." All this, though I loved music with a romantic passion. The passion is still burning.

After my first semester in college, I had my last discussion about a musical career with my father. I was asleep one morning when he awakened me. He had in his hand what looked like a blueprint. It was my college report card. He spoke.

"Here, Genius, here is your diploma." I looked at the list of subjects. They blurred. I saw a lot of "A's." But there, big and black, was an "E," that horrifying letter which signifies academic doom. The "E" was in math. I had managed to flunk math, a simple, snap course that was thrown into the curriculum because a minimum amount of that discipline was mandatory in the Liberal Arts school at Temple. Mandatory or not, I hadn't given a damn about it and had barely opened the text, thinking I was smart enough to cram for the whole course in the week before the final. I wasn't. Joseph S. Toobin said I was through.

"You're through," he said.

Then, suddenly, wildly, he stamped out of the room and came stamping back carrying a pile of pocket scores I kept on the piano.

"This crap goes out the window." He was seething. He held the scores high as though they would contaminate anything they touched. "I'm throwing this crap out. It's making a bum out of you."

Well, the scores didn't go out the window. They went back to the Free Library of Philadelphia, where they were long overdue. And if I was "through," I don't know exactly how that manifested itself. I went back to Temple, I made up the math in extra time, and I graduated with a B.A. in nothing in particular. English, that is. To the end, my father thought that I would come to my senses and, the B.A. gained, go on to professional school —law or medicine. I guess even *he* couldn't see me as a dentist. My career as an active musician was over. Only the romantic passion remained. It is not enough with which to serve the great art of music. I will always regret that I could not really serve it.

I did not take my B.A. in nothing in particular to a professional school; I took it to the Army Air Force. The war allowed me to defer the decision on what to do with myself for almost three years. I was an enlisted man and later became a lieutenant in the Troop Carrier Command, the folks that carried the paratroopers around. In my last year of service I worked with the first units concerned with air evacuation of wounded. The C-47 plane, which carried paratroopers, was easily convertible into a huge air ambulance, and I was in on the pioneering days of its use.

The service was no trauma to me. I never came anywhere near enemy fire. I shocked friends and relatives (and myself above all) by being a reasonably competent soldier. I saw some of the world: every nook and cranny of the sunny, steamy state of Florida; a corner of North Africa; a little of Sicily. I was wounded at the end of my military career, but in a most unheroic manner. Having been returned to the United States to train others in the by then burgeoning procedure of evacuating battle casualties by air, I was on my way from Alliance, Nebraska, to Philadelphia on a weekend leave when the C-47 I was in skidded on a runway at what was then Langley Field, near Washington, D.C. We were making a stop to deliver an armchair general to his armchair. I was hurt badly enough to warrant a discharge in late 1944. The war effort survived this disaster.

Back home, I literally drifted into my first job. I worked as a public-relations officer for the National Labor Relations Board, an agency which was noteworthy for its progressive role in the great days of the New

Deal. A concern for politics—and many other important concerns in my intellectual life—dated from my thirteenth year when I had fallen under the influence of a remarkable man, Louis Kay, the owner of a printing establishment in Philadelphia, and the father of Hershy Kay, a lifelong friend and today a famous arranger and the composer of some Balanchine ballets. Louis Kay talked politics to me, told me what to read, analyzed, guided; I was what we called in those days a "progressive," which meant a liberal far to the left of today's species. Louis Kay also influenced my tastes in music and literature; my debt to him is incalculable, and I will never forget him.

The drift into a job was occasioned by my bumping into an old schoolmate on the street. Very comely she was. At Temple she had known that I was interested in political matters, and, by extension, in the labor movement, and she informed me in our curbstone conference about her work with the NLRB, and how happy she thought I would be if I joined her. I repeat, she was very comely. I had been sequestered from her ilk for a long time. I was willing to join her almost anywhere. And while I had some interest in the work of the NLRB, joining it wasn't a hard-reasoned decision.

And an interesting job it was, too. In late 1945 and early 1946, I was assigned to the activities accompanying the CIO textile workers' attempts to organize the South for the first time on a mass basis. It was called "Operation Dixie." I was stationed in Chattanooga, Tennessee, most of the time. There, I cultivated the strongly ambivalent feelings toward the South that are common to so many Northerners; there were so many warm, humorous, delightful folks, with social philosophies that had changed little since the days of Jefferson Davis. My socializing with blacks, on the rare occasions when I had the opportunity, was looked on as an aberration induced by mental ailments brought on by the climate of Philadelphia. The white Southerners assured me that I would recover when I had been exposed to enough members of the black race. I just hadn't met the right—that is, the wrong—ones. That I had gone to completely integrated schools (Overbrook High School, alma mater of Wilt Chamberlain. What ever happened to him?) and that some of my friends were black eluded their comprehension. But they were tolerant. After all, as a Jew, I was congenitally peculiar, and they guessed I would "just have to learn the hard way." They tried instruction. I was regaled with depth analyses of black depravity, and all these exegeses would end with sinister accounts of black lust, and, so help me, the historical query as to whether I would allow my sister to marry one. My sister, then twenty-three or so, still unmarried and thus assured by our grandmother that she was doomed to spinsterhood, was actually fairly receptive to the idea. She could love both fair and brown.

In late 1946 the Taft-Hartley law was passed, and it looked to me as though the NLRB would change from an organization of arbitration to a policeman for industry. So I left.

My amorphous education made me a perfect candidate for service in that considerable company of *Luftmenschen* who float in the rarefied atmosphere known as public relations. I had good-paying, inconsequential jobs with establishment keystones, nay, rocks, like the Prudential Life Insurance Company, and lesser entities. All I remember about those days were glossy campaigns for glorifying products or for selling policies I knew nothing about. I was unencumbered by scruples. My glibness helped. There were long lunches in which my limited capacity for strong drink made it impossible for me to be one of the boys. I entered into a bad marriage with a lady who probably deserved better. So back in 1953 or 1954 I was going nowhere and had accomplished nothing. And I knew it, and I was—you said it, Henry—quietly desperate. But again, a walk on the historically seedy streets of Philadelphia changed my destiny. This time music was involved.

When I took this fateful walk I was out of touch with the music business almost entirely. My passion persisted, I went to concerts, I heard records, I conducted superbly in my imagination, and I still puttered with "that crap," scores and such. But I felt certain that I was never going to do anything about it. When, lo, as I was looking in the window of a record store on Walnut Street, I was poked in the ribs by a medium-sized fellow, swarthy, great shock of dark hair, familiar looking.

"Look at you!" he began. "You're—you're—hey, who are you?"

I told him. The fellow was in town with his new show, a musical called *Wonderful Town*. He was the composer of the show. His name was Leonard Bernstein. We went into a bar on Ninth Street. I told him something of what had happened to me since I had known him very casually at Curtis, when he was a promising piano and composition student—no conducting in *his* curriculum—and I was a little kid studying the fiddle with Luboshutz. Bernstein even as a student was something of a lion, and I was an obscure, skinny hanger-on who doted on a word from one of the mighty. Bernstein would occasionally throw me such a word.

Bernstein listened to my insubstantial, somewhat expurgated account, looking faintly amused, and finally interrupted. "That's all shit. Why the hell don't you get back into music?"

Well, this would take some doing because I had never really been *in* it. He suggested that I go up to Tanglewood that summer and offered to help get me a menial job on the faculty. So I taught a primitive course in music history for beginners in a program for nonprofessionals: Tanglewood's Group IV course for dilettantes who were trying to be part of the larger scene at that musical Mecca. And my life was pretty well turned around.

At the end of that summer of 1952, I was very grateful to Bernstein. I have had mixed feelings in the ensuing years. Oh, that bar on seedy Ninth Street!

Back in Philadelphia, with the Tanglewood experience, sparse though it was, to my credit, I used it as a selling point and got a job as assistant to the station manager of a "good music station," as all the nationwide imitators of WQXR were called. I was qualified to help program and promote the station, but there were more odious functions to perform. The grisliest of these was trying to sell radio time to the merchants of Philadelphia. The cultural fare of the station made it something less than an advertiser's dream. I was forced to seek out exotic boutiques, rare furniture dealers, and impoverished booksellers. Now and then I would find a real honest-to-god tycoon, whose climbing wife thought that the old man should be associated with the "finer things" in town—after all, the station did carry Phila-

delphia Orchestra concerts and that nice Mr. Ormandy
was always being interviewed (often by the salesman
himself). But I was a terrible salesman. And the tycoons
generally hated me after the first exchange of pleasan-
tries, if that late. Often, on my return to the office, the
Boss was waiting for me with horrendous accounts of
telephone callers who wanted to report the snotty, over-
bearing conduct of the "salesman" who had been un-
wisely dispatched to woo a local Croesus.

Quoth Croesus: "I don't owe you guys anything
whether you got Ormandy, Shmormandy, or what! It's
no privilege, believe me, doing business with that
smart-ass jerk you just sent over here. Just because he
likes music I don't have to waste my time hearing him
tell me how I should spend my hard-earned dough. He
isn't doing you any good. Keep him the hell out of here!"
Und so weiter. Since the manager and his wife were
climbers themselves, veritable Hillarys, in fact, you can
imagine my efficiency rating.

One nice thing about my life: I have always managed
to meet interesting characters wherever I landed. At the
radio station I met one of the greatest. He was a would-
be actor, the child of a psychiatrist connected with a
local hospital. The actor was obviously not going to stay
in Philadelphia; he trooped over to New York regularly
and was even taking courses at the Actor's Studio. We
often trooped over together, by bus. The station-manag-
ing Hillary was frugal, indeed cheaper than hell, and
even the bus was a strain. The actor was the early-morn-
ing announcer, and he was a good one. His name was
Mike Nichols. To be sure, he was unconventional; for
one thing, at 8:00 a.m. or so he would play some eye-

brow-raising poetry recording. I can still hear Dylan
Thomas magnificently intoning to our small but distinguished audience:

When I was a gusty man and a half
And the black beast of the beetles' pew,
(Sighed the old ram rod, dying of bitches). . . .

Well, either the manager and his wife and other
proper souls didn't listen that early or they were more
aesthetically advanced and tolerant than I suspected; at
any rate, the actor-announcer continued to beam those
marvelous and free-spirited words, strictly for grown-
ups. And the great music of course. Nichols and I went
to concerts and plays and tried poetry on each other, and
this kid—he was in his early twenties, just out of the
University of Chicago—was obviously something special. I remember one claim to fame he bragged about:
his grandmother (he was of German descent, indeed
had been born in Germany) had written the libretto for
Richard Strauss's *Salome*—though in reality it was just
a translation of Oscar Wilde's play. While he was in no
way self-effacing, I can't remember him as one for undue self-adulation.

But one unconventional habit of my friend's finally
did him in at the station. He lived in the center of Philadelphia, and the station was located far out in dismal if
grand-sounding Roxborough (8200 for any Philadelphians, which will lend dimension to the account of how
really far out it was). It was no mean chore to be out at
the studio at sign-on time, which was 7:00 a.m. Like all
little stations with frugal bosses, ours was a one-man
operation at sign-on time, and our announcer was also
engineer, administrator, receptionist, mail-sorter, and

so forth, until the nine o'clock arrival of the rest of the staff—both of them. Nichols tried; he took his dilapidated buggy out there to wildest Roxborough, and often he got there by seven o'clock. Sometimes he didn't, though, and therein lay his Waterloo—or his Roxborough.

For while Nichols may have been reasonably modest, he did have hubris where that most delicate of man's concepts is concerned: our announcer tampered with Time. Time, of course, is above and beyond all men; to try defying it is the ultimate imprudence of the human condition. But Mike Nichols tried, and like all men who think they can defy time, he perished; *stationwise,* that is, if I may so prove I was once in advertising.

How this hubris? Well, Mike would arrive at, let us say, 7:14 a.m. and sign on, cheerily, with a "Good morning, it's seven o'clock." Sometimes he arrived earlier—7:08—sometimes later—7:21—but he always spoke cheerfully and always said seven o'clock. In the sweet-natured morning of our announcer's soul it was always seven o'clock.

I knew about this "it's seven o'clock" business. So did some others. But none of the brass knew—for a while. There were two of those also, the manager and the station owner. This latter worthy, rich but, like many other old-line Philadelphia Quakers, from what source no one ever quite knew, had one claim to fame which he dragged out at the earliest opportunity: his brother had been married to Katharine Hepburn—for a very short time, to be sure, but all legal, with pictures in the *Bulletin* and *Inquirer* to prove it. And this was the station owner's conversational gemstone. It was not unusual to introduce Mr. Owner to a total stranger and have him say, "Harumph, how do ye do? Well, old Katharine Hepburn was once, ho ho, harumph, married to my brother, you know. Haven't seen old Kate lately." Neither had his brother.

Inevitably, the whilom brother-in-law of you know whom was destined to take an early train to New York, and on the way to the train he tuned his car radio to *his* station and he heard *his* announcer tell *his* audience that it was seven o'clock, when by *his* watch and a quick check of some other stations, it was well past seven fifteen. He drove right to the radio station, way out in Roxborough, and fired our announcer on the spot, at about eight thirty. Mike Nichols was no longer with us.

It was bound to happen. I never understood why the angry listeners, who jiggled their clocks and called the station (of course our announcer, being the only one on duty, would hardly report these complaints to the boss), never got the information of our announcer's misfeasances to the management. But they didn't, and there is no telling, had the owner not been on his way to New York on that fateful morning, how long those select few Philadelphians would have been regaled with the very highest level of pornography and the wrong time.

Mike was not unduly saddened by his precipitous ouster. He had other, bigger, sweeter fish to fry. He came to say good-by to me in my dusty old apartment on Locust Street, with a big announcement. He was going back to Chicago, he said, because he had gotten the part of Marchbanks in a Chicago equivalent of an Off-Broadway production of *Candide*. When I asked him how he had gotten it, he winked and, quoting the gangster in *The Great Gatsby,* merely said, "Gonnexions."

As he was leaving, he added, "Oh, yeah, did I tell you

about the night-club act I'm cooking up with that girl I
was telling you about? I don't know about that, but can
you imagine? Marchbanks!"

The girl he had been telling me about was Elaine
May. The announcer who tried to tamper with time has
certainly done all right. I don't know *what* he does about
the correct time these days.

It was General David Sarnoff of the Radio Corporation of America who took the next hand in changing my
life. On April 4, 1954, Arturo Toscanini conducted his
last concert with the NBC Symphony Orchestra, and
announced his retirement in a "Dear David" letter to
Sarnoff. I will never forget this period in the death of the
great orchestra the Maestro had molded, because I was
present, by chance, at the last rehearsal for the last concert. Through Don Gillis, producer of the NBC Symphony broadcasts, and a friend of my boss at the radio
station, I was admitted along with two hundred or so
others to this last of the NBC Symphony rehearsals.
There is a notion abroad that symphony rehearsals are
a sacred rite closed entirely to the public. Except for a
few ultra-secretive conductors, or conductors who are
treated contemptuously by their orchestras (and there
are more of this type than one might imagine) and don't
want to be made public spectacles of, most conductors
allow small groups of auditors to attend rehearsals, and
they particularly welcome students who stand to benefit
from watching experienced hands at work.

General Motors, the sponsor of the Maestro's last season on the air, invited two or three hundred people to
the last two rehearsals for each broadcast concert. The

amazing thing to me was that GM considered attending rehearsals less of a privilege than going to the concert. I knew this because the agency that dispensed the tickets for the Sunday afternoon Toscanini concerts always distributed the rehearsal passes *after* they had exhausted the supply for the concert and sent the rehearsal passes along with a note of apology. Astonishing —to apologize for alloting the enormous privilege of watching this great genius at work in the rehearsal hall, where the real work for the concert is done. It was with this group of "unfortunates" that I entered Carnegie Hall on April 3, 1954, for what was at that time only the "rumored" last rehearsal of Maestro and his orchestra.

I say "rumored," but there was little doubt in anyone's mind that this was the end of the glorious trail for the Maestro. So the tension as we awaited his entrance was greater than at any public event I have ever attended before or since. I was literally dizzy from it and felt as though I was going to pass out. This embarrassed me enough—what a way to say farewell to the Maestro—so that I managed to pull myself together and survived his coming.

Maestro walked slowly out, clutching the baton in his left hand, with which he also gripped his lapel. This was a common mannerism of his. I noticed first that he was wearing glasses—pince-nez—which was uncommon, though he wore them at home from time to time. They were virtually useless, actually, since his nearsightedness had been so bad from his youth onward that no optical devices were really helpful. Indeed his prodigious feats of memory, and they *were* fantastic, were occasioned, as he reminded his friends, by his terribly weak eyesight. Memorization was a must. He could never *see* a score, anyway. Many of his musicians tell without rancor of being introduced to him on the street "for the first time," after playing in the backstands of one of his string sections for a decade or longer. He could see only the first few stands, that is certain, but he could hear everything, and no one was safe whether Maestro knew what they looked like or not. His friends do report, however, that an exception to his dreadful vision was revealed in the case of beautiful women, whom he could spot at very great distances. This may be apocryphal. At any rate, Toscanini was wearing glasses when he came on stage for the last rehearsal, and I had never seen him do this in public before.

He mounted the plain railed wooden podium that he used and began immediately to work on the prelude to the first act of *Lohengrin*. The music sounded marvelous to me—soft, silken, the gradual crescendo perfectly modulated—but the Maestro seemed to be leaning back against the side of the podium, simply going through the motions. Even from my seat well back in the auditorium, I felt a lack of involvement, a preoccupation. In the middle of the piece I was startled to hear his voice —loud, harsh, quaking—uttering one word: *Intonazione* ("Intonation"). The piece progressed to its very soft, whispered conclusion.

He turned next to the *Waldweben* ("Forest Murmurs") from *Siegfried*. He said nothing, still beating time in an abstracted, detached manner. But the music sounded superb.

Now came "Siegfried's Rhine Journey" from *Götterdämmerung*. The same pattern I have described held for the first five or six minutes of this piece. Toscanini seemed almost lackadaisical in his conducting; it was hard to tell if he was hearing the music, so unchanging and mechanical was his beat. But suddenly, as the music reached the first of its great climaxes, he roared out —the only way I can describe it—"No! No! No! Timpani is too early. Too early. What you play! *Ignoranti! Porchi! Vergogna!* This music is the great passion—yes, the great passion of my life, and you spoil it! *Porchi! Vergogna!* Again. *Da capo!"*

There was obviously great perturbation and some confusion among the players. But they followed the direction and began the piece again. Toscanini was much more animated now in his conducting; he even seemed to be singing along very softly with the music. But as soon as the orchestra came to the passage that had caused the trouble the first time, there was a repetition of the outburst, only, if possible, more violent than the first time. Again the by now shrieked Italian imprecations. The voice no longer had its usual hoarse, rough quality: it was almost a scream. And after repeating *"Ignoranti"* and *"Vergogna"* over and over, he turned to his left, toward the first violins and said, in a much quieter tone, *"L'ultima prova"* ("the last rehearsal"), and walked rather quickly off the stage. Soon after, it was announced over the loud-speaker that the rehearsal was at an end. The stunned orchestra members and the small audience departed. The last rehearsal was over.

By the time I got out to Fifty-sixth Street—near the backstage entrance to Carnegie Hall—I saw that members of the orchestra were already leaving. I met a horn player whom I had known since my days as a boy in Philadelphia, and he was terribly depressed. For one thing, he told me, there was no assurance that Toscanini would conduct the final concert, scheduled for the next afternoon. In fact the NBC people had already alerted Erich Leinsdorf to the possibility that he might be called on to substitute. Leinsdorf would have one rehearsal the next morning. In addition to the trauma of the *ultima prova* was the fact that Toscanini's son's wife, a great favorite of Maestro's, had suffered a heart attack and was in critical condition. (She was to die in a week or so.) Finally, and the horn player was very reluctant to discuss this, the blowup was occasioned by a mistake—but it was Toscanini's. I had noticed at one point during the terrible scene that Frank Miller, the first cellist and Toscanini's special favorite among the players, had tried to talk to him and been rebuffed with an imperious gesture. He was trying tactfully to call Maestro's attention to his error. The horn player said that he felt that Toscanini was actually berating himself, and that his rage turned inward was all the more ferocious. He shook his head sadly and said it was a horrible climax to an already calamitous situation: a great conductor was coming to the end of a magnificent career in a horrendous manner, and a great orchestra was dying.

And then the horn player nodded toward a limousine parked in front of the stage entrance. I looked in and saw Arturo Toscanini, slumped low in one corner, his fist to his face, looking wildly distraught, truly in agony. I felt as though I had looked in on a deeply personal moment, and for some reason that I still can't explain, there was absolutely no one near that limousine, no one was seeing what I saw. But I was drawn to gaze at the old man—and what I saw was the ineffable tragedy of a great artist, my personal hero, the personification of what the civilized life was all about, ending his days in a profound misery, occasioned by the one defeat man must finally suffer. Time had run out. *"L'ultima prova."* The end. After all the triumphs, the ovations that had to be seen to be believed, the honors, the enormous self-satisfactions that he must have known, there he sat, looking as lonely and trapped as any human I have ever seen. He lived on almost another three years, but I always felt that Arturo Toscanini died that Saturday afternoon in New York.

Toscanini conducted his last concert the night after the ill-fated rehearsal, and it almost broke up in chaos when Maestro lost his place during a performance of the "Venusberg" music from *Tannhäuser*, and Guido Cantelli, in the control room, signaled for the concert to be taken off the air, and a recording of the Brahms First was actually aired for a few seconds. But the indomitable Toscanini quickly rallied, and the program was completed with no further incident. And it was a very respectable Wagner concert; by any standard but Toscanini's, it would have been a triumph. But Toscanini let his baton fall after the last measures—whether accidentally or as a symbolic gesture no one will ever know —and walked off the stage, never to return. He took no curtain calls. Still, he made one more appearance with the NBC, to complete a recording of *Aïda* that was in preparation. And he was in full command of his powers.

In the last year of his life, the Maestro's eyesight gave out almost completely, but he stubbornly refused to be helped around his huge house in Riverdale, and he still looked at scores—though what, if anything, he saw no one knows. He wept a great deal, always when talking about a favorite work, repeating bitterly that he would never conduct it again. He had always been superstitious, and according to his few intimates, the old man never really lost many of the attributes of the peasant that he was in many of the simple things in his life. When he lived past eighty-seven, the age at which Verdi had died, he told friends that he knew that he had been cursed for some specific sin which he would refuse to discuss. (Certainly the last two years of the old titan's life were thoroughly miserable.)

In the last months of his life, Toscanini was visited by Filippo Ghignatti, the English horn player of the Symphony of the Air, a musician with whom he had been associated since the early 1920s, at La Scala among other places. Indeed Toscanini had specifically requested him for the NBC. Ghignatti adored Maestro and enjoyed telling such tales as the one about the time in 1925 when Toscanini conducted a fabulous revival of Puccini's *Manon Lescaut* at La Scala, with Puccini present at the rehearsals. Toscanini was brusque with Puccini; he would call him not to ask for clarifications, but to admonish him, in front of the whole cast and orchestra, for errors in orchestration, or in vocal writing. To say the least, his attitude toward the composer was hardly reverent. Now in 1925, I dare say, Ghignatti revered Puccini above Toscanini, and he was deeply resentful of this attitude. One day, during a break, he took his courage in hand and approached the composer.

"Forgive me, Maestro," he began, "but I don't understand why you let Toscanini talk to you this way. This is your music, it is magnificent, the whole world loves it, and he treats you, forgive me, Maestro, a thousand times for saying it, like a messenger boy."

Puccini looked startled and answered, "But, my dear,

Toscanini is so much a better musician than I am that I must listen to everything he says. I always learn from him. What difference does it make how he talks? He is Toscanini. Please don't worry about me. We must all listen when he talks so that we can learn."

Anyway, Walter Toscanini invited Ghignatti to come to Riverdale to see his father, thinking that a comrade from the by now ancient days might cheer the old man. And Toscanini was delighted. He took Ghignatti's face in his hands, saying, "Ah, *caro,* you have been with me so long. And I was mean to you, wasn't I? Many times I was mean to you." And the Maestro wept.

Ghignatti, surprisingly, quickly agreed with Toscanini. "Yes, Maestro, you were very mean to me. Because you said, when you were angry with me, that I did not try hard enough. Perhaps I was not a good musician, perhaps I played bad oboe or English horn. But not try? For *you*? That was cruel." Ghignatti had character and simplicity of the best kind, and he told Toscanini what he felt, even though, as they both well knew, this was to be their last meeting.

Within a matter of hours after the Toscanini "retirement" and the announcement that the Toscanini Orchestra, as it was popularly and accurately called, was to be disbanded, the members of the orchestra were given six weeks' notice, and that was to be that. There was, naturally, a great deal of agitation both within and without the orchestra's ranks, and in less than a week, there were reports that the orchestra intended to stay alive, independent of General Sarnoff and his organization, and the structure of the reconstituted group was to be that of a cooperative ruled by a committee of member musicians. The chief administrative officer of the group was to be the radio producer of the NBC Symphony broadcasts, a minor Texas composer named Don Gillis.

I read of these doings in Philadelphia and, having all my conscious life been a fanatical admirer of Toscanini, was more than mildly interested. Certainly, my experience at the last rehearsal added any fillip that was necessary. I was convinced that it was a national artistic scandal for this great orchestra to be cut adrift and allowed to sink into oblivion.

But I knew very little about the actual workings of the new operation—only that it gave occasional concerts with guest conductors, was rumored to be attempting to negotiate recording contracts, and was showing the first symptoms of an organizational disease that was to rage through its body for all of its troubled life: dissent in the ranks. The cynical view is, I suppose, that this is often a concomitant of democracy, and that sometimes democracies make it and sometimes they don't. And an orchestral democracy is a particularly hazardous exemplar.

Very early it was announced that Gillis had left his post at the top of the organization. It was widely known that he had failed to get along with the orchestra's board and that no one in his right mind would ever succeed him. No one in his right mind ever did.

The orchestra was now known as the Symphony of the Air. All my information, later richly corroborated, showed that NBC was obstructing rather than assisting the orchestra's efforts to survive.

In the fall of 1954, the orchestra rented Carnegie Hall and performed one of the miraculous feats of American musical history, one which never received the approbation it deserved: a full-length *conductorless* concert.

The only direction was a nod of the head from the concertmaster, Daniel Guilet, as in a string quartet. The program, no simple affair, consisted of the Berlioz *Roman Carnival* Overture, Tchaikovsky's *Nutcracker Suite,* Wagner's *Meistersinger* Prelude, and Dvořák's *New World* Symphony. The masterly execution, the astonishing precision were tributes to the personnel of the orchestra, but above all to the training they had received under Toscanini. There were rapturous reviews, all of which decried the action of NBC in deciding to disband the orchestra. But in the show-business phrase, bitter and worldly, "no one threw money."

The existence of the Symphony of the Air was obviously a day-to-day proposition. But the orchestra members remained staunch and adopted a motto and rallying cry: "The Orchestra That Refused to Die." Already, though, key players were deserting the ranks, excellent offers being impossible to refuse and economic necessity being a constant. Attempts to obtain even token support from the Toscanini family failed. It has never been ascertained to my satisfaction how Toscanini felt about the orchestra's fight for life. Some say he was kept from knowing the facts of the struggle by his son, Walter, who was at that time an employee (as a consultant) of NBC.

A less charitable view was expressed to me by the astute, sophisticated Erich Leinsdorf. I repeat his assessment not in any way to demean the great conductor, but because in essence, I subscribe to Leinsdorf's view. After all, no one ever questioned Toscanini's great ego, and who, in God's name, ever had more reason for self-esteem in his work? At any rate, Leinsdorf told me, "Look, I don't know how Toscanini feels about this Symphony of the Air matter, but I'll tell you this. Old timers

have told me that he thought the Met should fold after
he left it fifty years ago. And he thought the Philharmonic should go out of business after he left in 1936.
And he never conceded that there even *was* a La Scala
when he wasn't there. So how do you think he must feel
about an orchestra that was *his* in the fullest sense of
the word. I wouldn't expect too much from the Tosca-
ninis."

And the Symphony of the Air got absolutely nothing.
The music world looked gloomily on as the orchestra
struggled, was sympathetic, and wouldn't put ten cents
into an insurance policy on its life.

One of the first fund-raising schemes for the orchestra was the issuance of the recording of the conductorless concert. Two LPs were released, one containing the
New World, the other the shorter works. An advertising
campaign was launched with borrowed and scrounged
funds, offering the record, by mail only, for a fifteen-
dollar contribution. (The orchestra had organized as a
nonprofit, cooperative corporation called the Symphony
Foundation of America. The contribution, which enti-
tled the supporter to the conductorless record, was thus
tax-exempt.) I received a notice of this campaign at the
radio station in Philadelphia and decided to do something about it. In addition to prevailing on my boss to
grant a sizable number of promotional spots to the venture (I threw out vague, completely baseless hints about
invitations to the Toscanini home to discuss further
moves to help the orchestra), I was even inspired to
make one of my few sales as an operative of the station:
I induced a local wine company to sponsor a series of
hour-long broadcasts featuring Toscanini recordings,
with an intermission feature devoted to publicizing the

Symphony of the Air and soliciting sales for the conductorless record. During these intermissions I personally
interviewed whatever musical celebrities were coming
through Philadelphia to give recitals, or play with the
orchestra, or visit family or friends or whatever. Most
were sincerely devoted to the idea of helping the Symphony of the Air stay alive, and graciously cooperated.

Eugene Ormandy, conductor of the Philadelphia Orchestra, made several appearances, which was no great
trick, since he loved being on the air, and even in our
regular programing was a regular, if not to say overfamiliar, fixture. If any time passed between Ormandy
appearances on the station, I was sure to get a call from
the conductor or one of his staff—usually it was the
conductor—asking if he had offended me in any way. I
was always astounded at how this musician, a very good
one, who had risen to one of the key positions in the
whole international musical scene, from the Capitol
Theatre Orchestra, by the way, acted in this obsequious
manner, which embarrassed me no end.

Once, after Ormandy had not been invited for almost
a fortnight, he called me with what was surely a pretext:
"Tell me, Jerry, what do you hear about Toscanini's
health? I've heard bad reports." I hadn't heard any, and
before I could get too alarmed, Ormandy continued,
"Tell me the truth, Jerry, you are one of my best friends
in the city. [!!!] I am really a bad radio guest, no? I think
you didn't like what I said about . . ." And so on.

So I said, "Not at all, Gene. It was fine. How about next
Friday before the concert? You can talk about the
Brahms program." And talk he did next Friday, and
while Brahms scholarship didn't retrogress too much, it

certainly didn't advance much either.

Another time, when Ormandy was raving about how much Toscanini had inspired him, he gave me an interesting insight into how Toscanini thought on domestic matters. "You know, Jerry, Maestro has never invited me to Riverdale any more since my divorce. He absolutely refuses to have divorced people as social guests. He is a great believer in the family. So I am out." (I heard this other places, too. Toscanini was by no means prudish; he felt that an occasional mistress was perfectly acceptable to maintain the artist's creative ardor. But divorce was absolutely out, and Ormandy was by no means the only musician banished from the Toscanini circle for violating the marital code. And this had nothing whatever to do with Catholicism, because Toscanini was an outspoken foe of the Vatican and would berate any pope you mentioned from the Middle Ages to last week.)

And so I began to raise funds for the Symphony of the Air in Philadelphia. I was unusually successful, and I never understood why. Perhaps it was underdog sympathy engendered by the famous orchestra sacked by the huge commercial empire; or perhaps it was the appeal of the record with its unique conductorless aspect; or perhaps it was a late manifestation of the Toscanini charisma. At any rate the checks began to roll in, and before the thirteen weeks of the first radio series was over, we had sent over fifteen thousand dollars to Symphony of the Air headquarters in Carnegie Hall. This return continued at the same pace for the second thirteen-week series. I was quite overwhelmed (as were, to put it mildly, the Symphony people) because we had expected at best a small, steady response, but nothing like thirty thousand dollars. It was, alas, one of my very few financial coups.

Understandably, I was fast becoming a hero to the orchestral management, and my correspondence file was bulging with enthusiastic notes from musicians I had respected from afar since my student days. But, strangely, I never went to New York to meet my new-found admirers. For some reason (perhaps it was a fore-boding of my rational self), I was very reluctant to meet the powers-that-be at the Symphony of the Air. It was becoming a musical affair à la Tchaikovsky and Nadejda von Meck. But Renata Tebaldi changed all that.

Tebaldi was then—in 1955—at the beginning of her career in America. She was well known to record collec-tors, and her reputation was building, but she was still not really famous, at least in Philadelphia. Some friends of mine, who were backing stray musical events from time to time in Philadelphia, booked Tebaldi for a re-cital. The house was scaled much too high, Tebaldi still lacked a popular image, and after a month of promoting the concert, the impresarios had sold only a handful of tickets.

Only four weeks remained before the concert, cancel-lation was contemplated, disaster seemed assured. The backers asked me for a specialized kind of help. What they proposed was that I go to New York and do an interview with Tebaldi. We knew that she spoke practi-cally no English, but they thought to turn this into an asset. I would use an interpreter—the promoters had ascertained through her management that Tebaldi's secretary would fulfill that function—and by having

Tebaldi speak in Italian could aim the interview at the Italian-language stations in Philadelphia, many of which still flourished in those days. It is an indisputable fact (or was in those ancient times) that the hard-core Italian opera lovers of a community spelled life or death for any operatic venture (so long as it wasn't Wagner, that is).

I agreed to the interview project, but there was one small problem when I alighted in New York. I had forgotten to bring a tape recorder. But that was easy. Tebaldi lived in the Hotel Buckingham, traditional home-away-from-home for Italian opera singers, and across the street from Carnegie Hall. I would stop in the offices of the Symphony of the Air, where I would undoubtedly find a tape recorder. Also, I would finally meet some of my pen pals. Actually, I neurotically hoped that very few would be present while I was making my visit. When I got to the office many of the musicians were about. I was greeted warmly, I was lent a tape recorder, and I promised to come back after the Tebaldi interview for a chat. The interview went well, I fell in love with Tebaldi for almost a week, and I chatted with the men of the Symphony of the Air. Two hours later it was decided that I would move to New York and go to work for the Symphony. It all happened quite casually, as though it was understood on both sides that it was inevitable that it would happen. Maybe it was.

Nine years later when, broke and dispirited, I left the Symphony, I again walked up Fifty-seventh Street and remembered the soaring feeling of exultation I had known that day long ago when I had come to interview Tebaldi. There I was—young and healthy and creative —working for Toscanini—almost. I would be the savior

of his orchestra—me, Jerry Toobin out of Philadelphia,
who loved the Maestro both sides of idolatry. And who
loved music even more. Oh yes, I soared down Fifty-
seventh Street that freezing December day in 1955. I
was Toscanini's man. I was unstoppable.

But I was very stoppable. The succeeding pages will
record how completely stoppable I was. It is a case history of what the business of music can do to the inno-
cent, the overly romantic, the unbusinesslike, when
they try to breach its dollar-lined fortress. Poor Renata.
I always blamed her, in a way, for my dire end as a
musical personnage. To add insult—my interview
helped very little. Renata sang to a half-empty house.

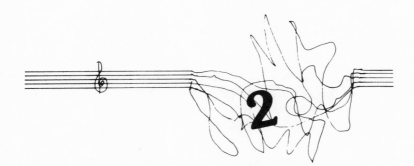

While my home was by no means a beehive
of culture, there was cultural talk, of a sort, going back
generally to my parents' courtship days. There were
reminiscences of Geraldine Farrar in *Carmen* and Feo-
dor Chaliapin in *Boris Godunov,* but always there was
Stokowski. (Pronounced right, too, Sta-kuff-ski; "no cow
in my name," the maestro would mutter to some well-
meaning adulator with insufficient knowledge.)

Naturally it was my mother who spoke most about the
"blond maestro," as the press dubbed him when he was
still sort of blond. Platinum blond is what he was when
I first saw him back in the early 1930s. Tillie Toobin was
a Stokowski fan from the first I can remember, and the
first I can remember is a ten-inch disc of the Brahms
Fifth Hungarian Dance played, tinnily, by the Philadelphia Orchestra and Stokowski. I must have been five or
so when they played it for me, and I can hear it now,
coming out of a bulky old phonograph which had to be
rewound, laboriously, after every side. And that record,
three minutes or so in duration, would start my mother
off on a series of raves about how handsome Stokowski
had been (even in 1930 he was considered an aging
idol), and how he had sent the women (it was always the
women) in his audience into ecstasy, and how he would

lecture latecomers and talkers. This was always the peak of the account: how he would turn to the audience as latecomers were scurrying seatward, and sarcastically, ironically, eyebrow-liftingly, scourge them. "Who sent for you, please?" or, "Are we disturbing you?" or, "We'll wait." I always thought these flashes of Stokowskian ire were pretty flat, but I never dared infringe on my mother's excited reminiscences. Lord knows she had few enough of them. The climax came when she said, and she said it endlessly, "Oh, was he a matinee idol!"

So Stokowski was a household word from the first day in my home, and certainly when I went out into the reasonably wide world of Philadelphia, there was no surcease, because Stokowski was—with the possible exception of Connie Mack, then managing the last of the great Philadelphia Athletics teams—our premier celebrity. I don't remember the first time I saw Stokowski in the flesh, and again my mother's reminiscences take over. She took me, apparently, at age four to a children's concert in the Philadelphia Academy of Music, home of the orchestra to this day, Stokowski conducting.

Her account: "I carried Jerome all the way up to the Amphitheatre [peanut gallery, Philadelphia style], and God knows he weighed a ton. They were playing the *Carnival of the Animals,* and they had real elephants on the stage. But my Jerome slept through the whole thing. Who would have thought he would turn out so musical!"

Well, I don't know how musical I turned out, but I don't remember anything of that event—no Stokowski, no elephants, no being carried up to the Amphitheatre, no sleep, and no weighing a ton.

When I started attending Philadelphia Orchestra concerts in about 1934, when I was twelve, Stokowski was the Father, the Son, and all the stars and planets and constellations thrown in for good measure. He drew great sounds from that outfit, astonishing sounds: the Stokowski sound. And he looked great: slim, imperious, the famous hands making patterns of sorts. I never really discerned much of a beat, and most musicians I have talked to agreed. But on nine or ten programs of that period, I wrote, "This was the greatest program I ever heard in my life."

Many years later, I was talking to Bruno Walter about conductors, and when Stokowski's name came up, he laughed quietly, and snorted a little. "Ah, Stokowski——" he began.

"Well, Dr. Walter," I interrupted, "I should tell you that Stokowski was my great hero when I was in my teens. I thought he was the greatest conductor in the world."

"But my dear," Walter quickly answered, "when you are fifteen, Stokowski *should* be the greatest conductor in the world."

Stokowski had instituted in Philadelphia what he called the Youth Movement, with concerts five times a year for audiences thirteen to twenty-five years old. Stokowski did a tremendous amount of promotion of music for young listeners in Philadelphia, even if some infants in arms slept through concerts, and even though some Rittenhouse Square cynics sneered that it was an elaborate method for Stokowski to meet young girls. Musical interest in Philadelphia was always at a high pitch. The subscription sale took all but three hundred or so seats in the Amphitheatre, which sold for fifty cents. They were put on sale at 7:45 on Saturday nights, and if you weren't in line by noon, you could forget about them. And when something special came up (Rachmaninoff— I heard the very first performance of the *Rhapsody on a Theme of Paganini;* or Kreisler playing the Brahms Violin Concerto and looking more aristocratic than the Margrave of Brandenburg, who, I assume, looked aristocratic; or one of Stokowski's specials, like a horribly truncated *St. Matthew Passion,* which he squeezed into the regular hour-and-a-half concert time. "Ah, my dear, when you are fifteen . . ."), you had to be there very early in the morning, and twelve noon could be too late. There was a peculiar danger to standing in that line; namely, a colony of pigeons perched on the Academy roof. An umbrella was not amiss in any kind of weather on the line in Philadelphia.

I enlisted in the Youth Movement, circa 1935, just short of the lower limit of thirteen, and dreaded that some bureaucrat in the orchestra organization would ask for a birth certificate to establish my right to serve in Stokowski's blessed ranks. My exalted position was that of usher and age verifier, for Stokowski insisted that no one over twenty-five (or under thirteen, alas) could be admitted through the portals on Youth Concert night. I served in a minuscule role in World War II, and I managed a symphony orchestra, and I dealt with officials of the musicians' union—in short, I have known some peril in my day. But nothing compared with going up to some lady (and at thirteen one has a very under-developed idea of age) and saying, "Pardon me, Ma'am, but are you over twenty-five?" Especially, since I considered twenty-five hardening-of-the-arteries country, and something shameful, like baldness, or being a Republican. "Young man, don't be impertinent," said one indignant Main Line debutante. "Go to hell, you little worm," said a lady who lived in our neighborhood and thought my question disloyal, as well as brazen.

But the concerts were really something—no playing down at all, every program the same type the subscribers heard. And as I grew older, I rose in the echelons of Stokowski's youth army. I keep referring to him as Stokowski, but certainly few others in Philadelphia ever did. He was always Stoki. And if I so refer to him, it is only because everybody did.

I liked writing, and early in my career with the Youth Movement I began to send in program notes for the program book that was put together for each concert. The Youth Movement did everything for these concerts —posters, decorations, the grisly ushering previously described, the program, everything. And as soloist for each concert, Stoki chose an instrumentalist or singer from the thirteen to twenty-five bracket. Many a big musical name made his debut at the Youth Concerts, and it was a cherished engagement.

My notes were fairly good and I was assiduous, so that by the time I was fourteen I was the leading contributor to the program. And one day came my reward.

Our family telephone was in the booth at the back of my father's drugstore. I was out playing punchball in the street one late summer afternoon (punchball being one of the endless variants of baseball I indulged in) when my father called that I was wanted on the phone. This was already an event of no small moment, since in my milieu phone calls were pretty rare in the afternoon, the telephone coming into use only after dark for homework consultations and hesitant conversations with girls one wouldn't dream of approaching in person. At least I wouldn't, but I *was* quite a Lothario in front of a receiver.

The call was from the head of the Youth Committee, the Youth Movement's politburo, with a division head for each department—posters, ushering, program, and so forth. This ruling group of five or six Main Liners usually ran the whole show, responsible directly to Stoki.

The executive who called me was very Main Line, and his diction and manner scared the hell out of me. "Mr. Toobin [every letter pronounced, it seemed—even the two oo's], this is [inaudible] from the Youth Committee. We would like to talk to you about joining us to supervise program notes." Some words were clear as crystal; some I didn't get at all.

I was pleased and terrified at once because you don't usually get called in from playing center field in a punchball game to be offered a place on the politburo. But I listened on.

"Could you come by tomorrow evening about eight? We're meeting at the 'Aht Allah.' "

Now I didn't know what or where or if the "Aht Allah" was. But I wouldn't dare ask so mundane a question as, "What was that?" or, "What?" I gulped, "Thank you, I'll be there," and was about to gulp, "Thank you," again, when I heard the blessed click on the other end.

So there I was with the greatest single honor of my life (superseding, I suppose, having shaken hands with Jimmy Foxx after an Athletics game), and no clear idea at all where the honor was to be conferred. I won't belabor the way I found out that the "Aht Allah" was the Art Alliance, a Philadelphia cultural hangout where the elite met to carve out Philadelphia's aesthetic empires, but I found out, and I went, and I joined the committee as Commissar for Program Notes. There, I got my first real taste of class distinction. There were other "Aht Allahs" to decipher, there were problems of apparel and name droppings and, "What does your father do?" But I stuck it out. And I met Stoki!

Yes, I met Stoki. Now in this blasé age it may sound faintly ludicrous to describe my ecstasy at standing in the presence of this musical nonpareil. But the emotion and self-consciousness were both overwhelming. I still feel the tense, stomach-tightening sensations all these years later.

And did I once see Stoki plain, and did I stop and talk with him? You bet your life!

STOKI: What do you do?

J.T.: Program notes. I write program notes. I'm——

STOKI (obviously not having heard a word I said): Next yeah [the Stokowski accent—indescribably arcane, redolent of extreme exoticism—but after years of study the conclusion is that in essence it is—*mirabile dictu*—cockney] we will have a new guest conductor for the or-kés-tra. [Stoki always, always said or-kés-tra.] Do you know him? Ow-gay-na Or-mahn-dee.

Now I never heard of "Ow-gay-na Or-mahn-dee." But does a neophyte ask the pope, "Who's that?" Nor did I. That he was referring to Eugene Ormandy, of whom I *had* heard, didn't vitiate the magic of the moment. I had chatted—sort of—with Stoki.

Another time he asked me what I thought of Hindu dance. Before I answered—and it would not have been much of an answer—he continued, "You must see Uday Shankar. He's wahn-dah-fooll. [Stoki always, always said wahn-dah-fooll.] I knew him in India." There, I really almost fainted dead away. Vertigo set in. Not only Stoki in front of me, but he had been to India! India! Who, among mortals—Philadelphia mortals—ever had been to India?

Stokowski was certainly a hero of my youth.

I worked very closely with Stokowski when I managed the Symphony of the Air in New York for the period 1955–1963. When I came to New York to manage the orchestra in 1955, Stoki wasn't doing much. He was conducting in Houston (which he pronounced Hoo-ston), where, though he had the title of music director, he worked only a few weeks in the fall and spring. Because of the hero worship previously described, and because the Symphony of the Air needed some connections with name conductors, I immediately sought him out, without any illusions that he would remember me from Philadelphia. I was completely correct. He hadn't yet gone back to Philadelphia to conduct the orchestra as a guest (he finally did in 1961), and he didn't want to talk about Philadelphia. But he did want to conduct in New York, and he made no bones about it. Stoki was rarely diffident about anything he really wanted.

"If you want something very badly, you must try very hard for it," he once told me. "Remember that when you see some wahn-dah-fooll woman you desire." This was in 1960. If the reference books are correct, he was seventy-eight.

The orchestra's attitude toward Stokowski, though, was not very helpful. The feeling toward him reflected Toscanini's. To be sure, in the 1940s Toscanini had ostensibly agreed to Stokowski as co-conductor of the NBC Symphony. But no one could ever figure out what had induced Toscanini to make this decision, if indeed he had made it. The last time I ever heard about the Toscanini-Stokowski relationship was from Guido Cantelli, and he probably summed it up best.

Cantelli told me of being in Riverdale with Toscanini in 1956. Maestro, in a typically grumpy mood, was decrying the lack of conductorial talent around. "Eh, Guido," he asked, "Stokowski! He still conducts?"

"Yes, Maestro."

"Pagliaccio!" snorted the Maestro before the answer was out.

But whether it liked Stokowski or not, the orchestra needed him for his name and his contacts, particularly with recording companies. Recordings were the most lucrative source of income for our personnel. Stokowski still made records regularly, though I could never get much of a picture of how they sold. He certainly was no box-office draw in New York any more, as occasional concerts proved, and young audiences didn't remember the glory days of the 1920s and 1930s, when along with Toscanini and Koussevitzky he made up the great triumvirate. Then you could hardly get a ticket for a Philadelphia Orchestra concert anywhere it was given; by the 1950s Stokowski played to half-empty houses in New York. In Europe where he guest-conducted rarely even in his greatest days, he continued to draw well, because curiosity over his great reputation persisted. European critics generally failed to find anything in particular to justify that reputation. I think they were wrong.

Stoki was living in 1956 in a huge, almost completely unfurnished Fifth Avenue apartment, with a magnificent view of the park, though in many hours spent there

with him, I never once saw him look out the great pic-
ture-window. There was an oriental gong—anywhere
Stoki went there was an oriental gong. And a weird
clock of his own design, constructed on the wall in back
of where he worked, which my mechanical illiteracy
kept me from understanding. Suffice it to say, it had only
a minute hand.

He worked at a long, narrow work table which he
seemed to surround, peering very closely at the material
that was before him. He looked very much like a great
bird poised over the sheets of music, and I never really
knew whether it was nearsightedness or ferocious concentration that kept him so poised. Certainly Stoki
wouldn't wear eyeglasses! He would, when I was ushered into the presence, continue to peer down at the
music or whatever, and say, "Just a moment, please."
Always the ferocious concentration, always the hawk-
like attention to what was before him, always the slight
delay while he finished his communion with whatever
it was. Occasionally it was not music, and it was slightly
disillusioning once, snooping as I sat before him, to see
that it was a Con Edison bill. On another, more memorable visit, I was ushered in by a secretary. (He changed
secretaries every few months, alternating the very
lovely with the most incredibly ill favored.) He was on
the phone, and what I heard was: "One pound of hahm-
boor-ger. One box of—what you call it—cleanser." And
so on. The conductor was ordering the groceries. *Sic
transit gloria.* This was the same supernatural being
who had been to India and exuded the deepest mystery
and glamour when he walked across a room to shake
hands with an earthbound adolescent from West Philadelphia.

Stokowski, when I first worked with him in New York, wasn't very busy at all. One indiscreet secretary—ill favored—told me that he would call her in for dictation and then proceed to dictate a note to go with every bill he was paying, including a missive to the aforementioned Con Edison complaining about the quality of its lighting. He was probably right, too. But he had to keep up the illusion at least of working continuously.

If I'm giving the impression that I attained any real intimacy with Stokowski, I'm being misleading. I just spent quite a bit of time with him, and certainly began to perceive what he was like, and how, I suspect, he always was.

I mentioned the reference books. Encyclopedias, dictionaries, musical histories give—or at least gave, until about ten years ago—1882 as the year of his birth. If it was indeed 1882, it helps make it somewhat of an *annus mirabilis:* Joyce, Stravinsky, Franklin D. Roosevelt. But Stoki, sometime in the 1950s, began to insist on 1887. In fact, he rocked Miami Beach—at least such of it as was listening to a radio interview with him on a local station —by walking right out on the interviewer, when that unfortunate said, "Now, Maestro, you were born in 1882."

"Where did you get that information?" queried Stokowski.

"From the *World Almanac,*" said the interviewer.

"If that is the kind of information you have, I think I had better end this right now. Good aftahnoon." And he was gone.

The distraught radio man sat clutching his *World Almanac* and heaven knows what else, with twenty-nine minutes to go on a half-hour program. The *World Al-*

manac, along with every other reference book (until the late revision) did indeed give 1882.

Stoki had to be—granting even *his* date—near seventy-five when I renewed contact with him in 1956. And he looked it. His face was parchment pale, the skin flaccid; the famous hands very puffy; the eyes small and hawkish; the hair stringy and bluish gray. But he had an amazing knack for dressing up, and on concert nights or for special social occasions, he could *still* look like an aged, debauched, but very domineering grandee. The hair even, by some alchemy, would fluff out enough so that he bore some slight resemblance to the Stoki of my youth. The hands had indeed been puffy and swollen even in the great days when he had the lighting on the Philadelphia Academy stage adjusted so that their reflection was visible on the ceiling of the hall. The real reason Stoki began to conduct without a baton in the 1920s was the very unaesthetic one of a painful arthritis which made it most difficult for him to grip the stick. I had this corroborated for me by a doctor who, in his youth, had been an assistant to the specialist treating Stoki.

But Stokowski was not acting like any seventy-five. He was always planning ahead, always talking about a new or-kés-tra. The Symphony of the Air as then constituted never pleased him. The players—the oldest of whom was his junior by decades—were "too old." He was never reluctant to talk about other people getting old. But you had better never talk about the past to Stokowski. At least no longer back than five or six years.

Two incidents come to mind. Once, in 1956, Rose Bampton, the soprano, came into his dressing room, delighted to see him again after many years and said, a little gushingly for his taste (he hated gushing), "Dr. Stokowski, I was listening to the records we made in 1932 of the *Gurrelieder* and I think they're still fine. 1932!"

The repetition was unfortunate. Stoki sat quietly for what seemed like a long time. And—alas, poor Rose—there was a calendar on the wall. Stoki stood up suddenly, stalked to the wall, slammed his fist on the calendar, hard—so hard that I winced, knowing about the hands—and fairly shouted, "My God, woman, do you live by *that* thing!"

And the reunion was over.

Another time, an unctuous violinist in the front row of second fiddles, who was an art speculator on the side and who tried to ingratiate himself by name-dropping to art-conscious conductors, approached Stokowski at a rehearsal break and oozed, in his Hungarian accent, "Maestro, I found, yesterday, in an old scrapbook a picture of you and Kandinsky taken in nineteen hundred and fifteen!"

Stokowski looked at him, the eyebrow arched (the eyebrow almost always arched when he was annoyed), and said, "Have you looked at the music for the Bartok? It's very difficult, you know."

Stoki had no appetite for nostalgia, or sentiment about the past, and he never seemed to consider anyone as unduly important. When F. D. Roosevelt's name came up, he would say, "Oh, yes, Roosevelt, he was a friend of mine." Once, when we were playing summer concerts at Bear Mountain, Stokowski stayed at an inn in nearby West Point. He complained to me one morning that there had been bugles very early that had awakened him.

"Well, we must have generals, so we have to put up with West Point," I replied, fatuously. (I often spoke to Stoki with great self-consciousness, and an anthology of my conversations with him—at least my side of them—would be a treasury of inanities.)

"Oh, yes, generals," Stoki answered. "I knew a general once—what was his name? Mac—Mac—Mac something."

"MacArthur," assisted the indefatigably obtuse orchestra manager.

"That's it," conceded the conductor.

We were going through a list of proposed works for recording, and as he came to such "esoteric" and "far-out" names as Hindemith and Bartók (he was talking to professionals) he helpfully identified them. "There is Hindemith—he is a German composer. Bartók was a Hungarian composer who wrote very interesting and dramatic music."

He seemed to think that he was in sole possession of all sorts of information which had not yet burst on an unsuspecting world.

Once he called me at home to tell me about a United Nations concert he had been asked to give, in which he would introduce a Turkish score by that country's leading composer. My wife took the call in my absence and quoted him as follows: "There is a country. It is called Turkey. They have interesting music which is never played." And so on. She was a little taken aback by his opening sentences, which assumed, as it seemed, on her part, somewhat less than a consummate knowledge of geography. She insists to this day she *knew* there was a country named Turkey.

I've mentioned Stokowski's condescension toward the

"older" players. One of these "older players" precipitated a scandalous scene at a Symphony of the Air rehearsal in 1958 which, amazingly, didn't get much publicity, even though anyone who witnessed it is not likely ever to forget it.

I was forewarned of it.

The Symphony of the Air, suffering, quite often, from a very fluid personnel situation, needed a first trumpet player of experience and excellence for an American-music concert Stokowski was conducting. Earlier in our history we had utilized Toscanini's first trumpet—one of the greatest in the world—but he didn't like many things about the post-Toscanini days and didn't perform with us. I was always puzzled by this man, a great instrumentalist if there ever was one, a sentimentalist who wept at the memory of a kind word from Maestro, and who in real humility maintained that he sounded better with the Maestro conducting than he actually was. I sat with him as we listened to the Toscanini recording of Moussorgsky's *Pictures from an Exhibition,* and he kept shaking his head—no act here—and saying, "That's me, but I don't play that well."

Having heard that the trumpeter was talking to some colleague about wanting to play with the orchestra again, I suggested to the personnel manager that he approach him for the American-music concert. The trumpeter accepted the engagement, and I, deeply respectful of the man's unquestioned instrumental greatness, was overjoyed. The first thing I did at my daily conference with Stokowski was tell him the good news. Stokowski stared at me for a moment, coldly, and I knew instantly what was coming. "That is not good news. He is old. He played for me in Philadelphia [in the 1920s,

when the trumpeter was a boy]. But he is too old. This
is very difficult music. That is not good news."

Well, good news or not, the trumpeter was not disengaged; it would have been a cataclysmic union affair
had we tried to do so, and he appeared for rehearsal in
Carnegie Hall. Stokowski started right in. "I cannot
hear trumpet." Stokowski never used names—indeed
few virtuoso conductors ever did—only instruments.
And Stoki generally dispensed with articles. "Trumpet,
you are too loud. Trumpet, you are too soft. Trumpet,
please count, you are not together with us." Trumpet,
trumpet, trumpet, throughout the rehearsal.

Now the trumpeter had a notoriously low boiling
point. (He was the protagonist of one of the most famous
Toscanini stories: He was supposedly banished by the
Maestro for disputing an interpretative point and
shouted as he left, "And nuts to you, Maestro." The Maestro, never looking up, answered, "It'sa too late to apologize.") But he was very patient, very quiet at first. I felt
he was trying to follow Stokowski's instructions. After a
while it became obvious that more than instruction was
involved. The explosion came suddenly.

"Look, you goddamned has-been," the trumpeter began, "who the hell do you think you are?"

The one hundred men on stage, the ten people in the
audience, froze.

"This isn't Philadelphia thirty years ago," he continued. "And you're nobody. You has-been! Wake up;
you're nobody!"

Only one man seemed relaxed. Stokowski. He sat on
the high stool which he always had in back of him at
rehearsals. He kicked one leg lazily against it and, lei-
surely waving his hand at the trumpeter, repeated quite

a few times, "Good aftahnoon, suh. Good aftahnoon, suh."

Quickly unfrozen, the personnel manager made a beeline for the trumpeter and led him off, still yelling, though what I didn't hear. I just tried to get as low in my seat as possible with the ultimate objective of sinking through the floor and never surfacing again. Then I heard Stokowski say, quite amiably, "Mr. Too-been. Mr. Too-been. Can I see you a moment?"

Thinking quickly of the headline that night—ORCHES-TRA MANAGER SUFFERS STROKE AT STOKOWSKI REHEARSAL—I was starting to compose the next day's obit, with the irony of the childhood adoration of Stokowski and all, when I was before him, and he was still kicking the side of the stool, gently.

"Mr. Too-been, can you get that wahn-dah-fooll trumpet player who did the Wagner with us? You know, the big man. . . ."

No stroke, no obit; just Stoki sitting placidly on his stool, the only relaxed man on the stage. Stoki.

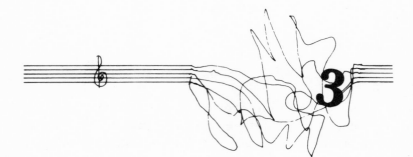

3

The closest I ever came to a personal relationship with Stokowski was at the time of the custody fight with his former wife, Gloria Vanderbilt, over their two sons. These lads—about ten and eight when the struggle took place in the late 50s—were Stoki's great "pride and joy" (his own phrase). They were handsome, ebullient kids, and one looked astonishingly like a photograph of Stokowski I had seen, taken not long after he came to Philadelphia in 1913. When the litigation over the boys broke, Stoki was in Europe, and he *flew* home. Stoki was always opposed to air travel, proclaiming planes "good things to stay out of." Actually he had had a traumatic experience in the early days of aviation the nature of which was not clear, but it kept him out of airplanes.

This time, however, his presence urgently needed in New York, he jetted home immediately. He called me to ask if I would testify on his behalf. Which I was happy to do because I had no qualms about Stoki as a father to the boys. Indeed, his patience and forbearance were such that I, no martinet with my own son, marvel in retrospect at his tolerance. I never heard him raise his voice to them, he endured calmly the usual endless questionings, and he seemed reasonably liberal with them, bikes and electric trains being among the few

objects discernible in the otherwise bleak and cavern-
ous apartment. It was a little odd, to be sure, to hear the
boys calling the patriarchal conductor "Dada," and I
had a hard time keeping a straight face when they
rushed at him one day yelling, "You made a boo-boo,
Dada." But the relationship was, to my mind, an excellent one, and I told the court just that in the brief appearance I was called on to make.

And the end of the case was pure Stokowski. "Try
harder, try harder" was a Stoki admonition to musicians. In the custody case he tried very hard indeed, and
in the face of his advanced age, state laws which are
generally favorable to the mother, and Miss Vanderbilt's (then Mrs. Lumet's) demonstrable ability to support the children adequately, he won a smashing victory. Stokowski could have the children for practically
50 per cent of the time and was granted the right to take
them on long vacations anywhere in the world. No lawyer I talked to understood it, but there it was, and I think
Stoki richly deserved the judgment.

While the case was going on, I talked to Stokowski a
good deal about family matters, and as usual his attitudes were noteworthy, if a bit strange. He expressed
himself this way on the marital state: "The woman always lives longer. [!] The man has worries all the time
about his business, and then he has—what you call it?
—the operation. And then he dies. And the woman gets
another husband."

Stoki's unique attitude toward time was manifested at
this juncture. "She, that woman I was married to, can't
keep those boys from me, no matter what happens. They
will grow older and they will know who is their real
friend. They will come to me, even if it is much later."

Naturally I could only do a little mental arithmetic, with astounding results. When they were twenty, he would be———. But Stoki was never cowed by statistics of probability, and he obviously saw himself spending the twilight of his years with his mature boys. When they were thirty . . .

I yearned to talk to Stoki about his own youth, but I just couldn't get up the nerve. I had heard stories about it, but no shred of corroboration to make them even worth repeating, though I must say I was intrigued by a story that his mother was still living in the 1950s and running a limousine service in London. Once, when complaining to me about Gloria Vanderbilt's inability to raise the boys well, he said that her great wealth was a hindrance, if anything. "I've led a busy life and I've worked hard. And I think I'm a good musician. And I was poor when I was as old as those boys are. Were you ever poor? [No wait for an answer, of course.] I was poorer than anyone you've ever known. Poorer than anyone." One of the few autobiographical notes I ever got from him.

Another, much more specific, came when I asked him if he liked Elgar's *Enigma* Variations. It is a favorite of mine, and I couldn't remember Stokowski ever programing it.

"I knew Elgar in England a long time ago. I knew a girl there, and she lived with another girl, and Elgar was in love with that other girl. She was a big, dark girl and she was hot. And Elgar would come see her when I was seeing the other girl, and he was embarrassed because of—well, Mrs. Elgar. I didn't care, but he was embarrassed. He was a very proper Englishman, you

know. And, oh, he loved that big girl. Then she went
away, and she died."

And he never did tell me if he liked the *Enigma*
Variations.

Stoki in England always brings to mind the "Leo
Stokes" business. For years there were reports that Stoki
was pure, straight English, with a very conventional
English background, who in the *fin-de-siècle* manner
took a foreign-sounding name to add to his aspiring
musical stature. Thus Leo Stokes became Leopold Stokowski (with the resounding middle names of Boleslawawicz Stanislaw Antoni thrown in for good measure). Stoki had been to Oxford, there is a record of that.
But I have seen what I consider decisive proof in the
name matter: an army citation made out to a grandfather, though at what remove was never made clear. I
couldn't make out the dates on the faded document. The
name on it was Leopold Boleslawawicz Stanislaw Antoni Stokowski. The same name as the conductor. I have
never understood why he showed it to me. Or do I?

I am certain that Stokowski was born Leopold Stokowski, and that he may have changed his name, for conve-
nience sake, during his student days in London, to Leo
Stokes. Stokowski was probably always the supremely
self-confident man I knew, and he didn't need a glamorous name or an unglamorous name. It once suited him
to be Leo Stokes, fine—but never unaware of the uses of
publicity and promotion, he had to realize that Leopold
Stokowski was a grand name for concert posters and,
after all, it *was* his. During the war, he conducted a
concert in New York to which the officers of H. M. S.
Hood were invited. One of them, seated next to a friend

of mine, said, "Oh, old Stokes. I was at Oxford with him." But I am certain it was, from the cradle, Stokowski.

Sean O'Casey has his "Paycock" Boyle say to his crony Joxer, in describing the unnaturally virtuous suitor of his daughter, "You know, Joxer, I never heard him usin' a curse."

Now I never suspected Stoki of natural or unnatural virtue—at least not in overdoses—but I never heard *him* (except once) "usin' a curse." His manner was genteel, and he was quite formal at all times. I was always Mr. Too-been to him, and it was a rare bird that he called by his first name. I can only think of the music publisher Oliver Daniel, whom Stoki called, rather juicily, O-lee-vayr. Actually he called women by their first names much more frequently, but then he had expressed himself often to me on their natural inferiority, "except for some things," he said with crude emphasis. Women, along with pets and servants, qualified for first-name treatment. He was given to authentic pronunciations, and always called my wife Mahr-lay-nah (Marlene), which, I daresay, took her a long way from her Shaker Heights, Ohio, beginnings. In fact, his authentic pronunciations often startled me. It was always Var-shav-a and Mos-kva, not Warsaw and Moscow, and more surprising, Cad-i-yac, for the automobile. But no obscenity ever and rarely even a mild expletive.

Once, in a very self-revealing outburst at the or-kés-tra, which he thought was being lethargic, he said, "If you don't want to play, all right. I don't give a damn. I'm the most independent man in the world." That "damn" was the strongest language I ever heard from Stoki.

And I guess he *was* the most independent man in the

world. Why he was is not too arcane a matter. He was
enormously successful, artistically and materially, almost from boyhood. By 1908 he was already music director of the Cincinnati Orchestra, then one of the greatest
in the country. He had already become something of a
luminary in New York, with his organ recitals at fash-
ionable St. Bartholomew's. One lady of my acquaint-
ance tells of her mother's stories of how the society
crème de la crème would gather on Sunday afternoons
at five at that Park Avenue shrine to hear Stokowski
play Bach—and to marvel at his youth and his good
looks. As he sat before the keyboards and charmed the
monied with the Passacaglia and the D Minor Toccata
and Fugue, I daresay he was turning over in his mind
the orchestral transcriptions which were to become one
of his great contributions to music. These days it is fash-
ionable to scoff at Stoki's reworkings and call them
unauthentic and falsifying. But they brought millions
of listeners some suggestion of the miraculous structure
and innate drama of Bach's organ music, then, in the
pre-LP days, practically inaccessible. *Pace,* Bruno Walter, I still admire them, at a great remove from age
fifteen.

Stokowski, at least into his seventies, had a career of
singular success, and while I don't purport to know how
he felt about his personal life, I somehow think he was
very content about things when I knew him. Once, on
Thanksgiving, we recorded the Brahms First Serenade,
and he told me, "I give thanks to Gawd for many things.
I have had children and two sons [*sic*], and I have made
music. But above all I give thanks for my good health.
That is the most important thing in life, and I've had it.
And I thank Gawd."

Stoki could never be accused of undue frivolity; in fact, he was about as humorless as anyone I ever met. In addition to never (except once) hearing a curse out of him, I also never heard an amusing story or a pun or anything even faintly funny. Occasionally he would be ironic, but this was most often heavy-handed, and he certainly never laughed at his own expense. He was once conducting a children's concert with the NBC, and, shades of my early shame, he was doing Saint-Saëns' *Carnival of the Animals.*

"Who knows what is a gee-rahff?" queried Stokowski. A little boy about eight raised his hand, jumped up, and cried, "A gee-rahff is a giraffe." Stoki never cracked a smile.

But worse, his approach to what passed for humor was often treacherous and led to dire consequences. Once, with the orchestra recording Resphigi's *Pines of Rome,* the session moved perilously close to its four-thirty conclusion, and the jittery personnel manager stood poised to tell Stokowski that fateful hour had struck and we were now on overtime. Union regulations. The moment came, the terrified personnel man motioned to him, Stokowski froze, gave him the most murderous look I've ever seen—and lowered his hands—and chuckled. Five or six years will be subtracted from that poor musician's allotted span for what Stoki thought were high jinks.

The Empire State Music Festival at Ellenville, New York, was the brainchild of Frank Forest, a frustrated tenor who had to be content with making millions in the pharmaceutical market. He was an amiable, handsome,

politico-looking fellow, and he had a deep desire to be
an impresario. He thought the Catskills, with their innumerable hotels and inns and other resort facilities,
would be an ideal recruiting ground for concert listeners, since, he assured me, "Jewish people love good music." Be that as it may, the festival died in a few seasons
because insufficient numbers of vacationers, Semitic or
not, could be lured from the bingo tables, floor shows,
1945 movies, and other cultural joys that embellished
the Catskill establishments. But in the first days, enthusiasm and optimism ran rampant. Forest found a nice
plot of land in Ellenville, pitched a huge tent on attractive, spacious grounds, and hired Stokowski to conduct
some special programs.

Stoki immediately had a large project in mind, and
only later research proved it to be as inappropriate for
the festival as Grossinger's would be for a Himmler
memorial meeting. The conductor chose for the season's major vehicle Carl Orff's incidental music for *A
Midsummer Night's Dream,* plus a complete staging of
the play. The cast included Basil Rathbone, Alvin Epstein (a wonderful Puck), Nancy Wickwire—and, as Bottom, Red Buttons. The Orff score had been composed for
German consumption after the Mendelssohn music was
proscribed for sensitive Aryan ears early in Hitler's
Third Reich. I don't really know if Stoki was aware of
this grisly fact, but I certainly wasn't when the production was scheduled, although why it didn't occur to me
is not to my credit. While the information was readily
accessible to anyone doing the least bit of research into
Orff's work, the only comment on his misbegotten *Midsummer Night's Dream* music was contained in a review by Winthrop Sargeant in *The New Yorker.*

But the production commenced and rehearsals—
many were scheduled—went well, until one fateful
night near the end of the preparation.

It was a very enterprising production that the festival
was putting on, and the director, Basil Langton, had
been resourceful in casting Buttons as Bottom. Red was
very successful on television at that period, and it was
thought that he would draw well in the Catskills. And he
was a quite effective Bottom—his bantam pomposity
and his Bronx-tinged English making for an unortho-
dox, but diverting, portrait of the weaver. He reminded
me of a young W. C. Fields, and I can think of no higher
praise. Rathbone was Rathbone; Nancy Wickwire was a
fine Titania; the always skillful Alvin Epstein, fresh
from his success in *Waiting for Godot,* was first rate as
Puck—everything was going fine. The music, what
there was of it, was harmless enough, just brief inter-
ludes really, and Stokowski was, for him, in a support-
ing role. But he seemed in a good enough humor.

The scene was act 3, scene 1, where Titania awakens
to the song of Bottom, now wearing his famous ass-head.
She falls instantly and crashingly in love with him, and
has her fairy court surround him. As part of their cod-
dling of Bottom-Buttons, the fairies presented him with
a banana. I wish they hadn't.

The sequence was repeated a few times, not many, but
Bottom-Buttons got a little bored. Up to then his conduct
had been exemplary. He had apparently worked very
hard in studying his role, and he was deadly serious
about its success. Certainly he hadn't done anything like
it in his burlesque-to-national-television odyssey, and
he was, I thought, the most dedicated member of the
cast. But it was pushing 11:00 p.m., it was muggy, the

atmosphere was relaxed, and Bottom-Buttons acted up. He took the banana the fairies had presented him with and, taking careful aim, threw it toward the open end—the bell—of the tuba in the orchestra pit. Stoki sat on his chromium stool before the orchestra. The Bottom-Buttons shot missed the bell of the tuba and ricocheted off the side into the lap of the tuba player. That helpful musician threw the banana back up to Red, and I looked at Stokowski. He was smiling, quietly smiling. Bottom-Buttons tried again. Perfect. Right in the bell. A smattering of applause. The cooperative tuba player plucked the banana out of the bell, and back up to Red it went. Stokowski chuckled. I saw him chuckle, I heard him chuckle. General giggling was taking over on stage, not raucous, just silly. And Bottom-Buttons aimed again at the tuba, when Stoki erupted.

"Stop this nawnsense! Stop it! Stop it! This is Shakespeare. This is Shakespeare, not vohdveel! This is not vohdveel! This is Shakespeare—the greatest. The greatest——" And here Stokowski started to splutter. Words failed, and he grunted the sound "Uh" and left the orchestra pit quickly.

Now this time I thought not of strokes and blessed deliverances like death—my death. Rather, in my hysteria, I thought chaotic fragmented thoughts which were, of course, coming up from my unconscious to delay the inevitable reality that Stoki was gone and someone had to bring him back. (I hadn't sat through Psych 1 and 2 at old Temple University for nothing.) I remember I kept thinking, "But vaudeville is dead!" And then, "And so is Shakespeare, the greatest——the greatest——" But the real world intruded too soon, in the suave British presence of director Langton.

"Well, Jerome, old boy, shall we have a go at it?" asked Langton.

I didn't answer, merely rose, and we had a go at it. Single file. Langton first.

Stoki was sitting backstage, perched on a trunk, and he was fuming. He was kicking the side of the trunk. (CARROLL MUSICAL INSTRUMENT COMPANY, it read. I was still blocking.)

Langton started, "Now, Maestro—see here——"

"Out!" screamed Stoki. "Out! Out!"

Three outs. End of the first half of the first. Home team coming to bat. I was by now hallucinating.

We went out. Me first. Now I began to cope—a little. I realized that Stoki was not given to walkouts. Toscanini, yes. Iconoclastic orchestra men said Toscanini's dramatic walkouts came generally when he was bored with a rehearsal, an eventuality which happened occasionally even to that giant. But Stoki had walked out, and I knew this was serious. After all, I stream-of-consciousnessed, he hadn't been in the papers in a long time. Also, he was only conducting snatches of continuity music, really. This would not have been the first time Stoki learned the score along with the executants, and maybe he hadn't realized the subordinate nature of the Orff music. Maybe. Perhaps. The fact remained that rehearsal time was wasting, and Stoki was on a trunk backstage, unapproachable. So I went back.

"Can I get you anything?" I queried.

Stoki didn't look up but began talking.

"I have just conducted in Wien [always the authentic pronunciation. Not too mad for that, I noted, hopefully]. Bear-leen. Hahm-boorg. [I thought of him ordering groceries. I was cracking under the strain.] Everywhere *aus-fer-kauft* ["sold-out" in German]. Everywhere. *Aus-ferkauft.* And here—this nawnsense. This vohdveel." Then again that "Uh," which seemed to synthesize all his anger and contempt and pent-up energy.

I was about to say something—useless, I'm sure—when the tent flap opened (this was, remember, a tent world and backstage was another part of the tent), and Red Buttons appeared. He looked little and scared, rather appealing. He walked up to Stoki and spoke.

"I'm sorry, Maestro, sorrier than I can say, believe me. I thought we were just fooling around a little. All the kids have been working so hard, and it's them I'm worried about. I just hope I haven't ruined everything for the kids."

My lunatic mind, still roaming, had transformed Red into James Cagney as George M. Cohan, although which scene in the movie epic I've never figured out.

"Come on, Maestro, let's shake hands. Please. For the kids."

Or was it Bob Hope as Eddie Foy? I was going mad!

Stoki's hand shot out. "Good. Let's shake hands. Now *you* get another conductor!"

Now *there* was a scene. Old Red sitting at a battered desk, clutching an old-fashioned stand-up telephone. "Hi, Pierre Monteux? This is Red Buttons." Or, "Operator, I want to place a person-to-person call to Mr. George Szell in Cleveland. My name is Buttons." Or Herbert von Karajan in Wien. Otto Klemperer in London. Charlie Munch in Boston. *He* was getting a new conductor—"for the kids."

Red just looked down. Defeated.

I moved in. "This is a very important production, Dr. Stokowski. When you suggested doing it [subtle, no?], I knew it would be difficult to do in so short a time. And it's been going so well till now."

"Yes, yes," interrupted Stoki, still banging away hard at the trunk with his British-mades. "That's why it is no time for nawnsense. Or vohdveel. No. No. I can't go on with this. Get another conductor. There are plenty of conductors." ("Hi, Bruno Walter? This is Red Buttons and Jerry Toobin.")

Now I reverted to my usual self with Stoki. "No, there is no other conductor here." That scintillating "here" had the proper doltish Toobin touch vis-à-vis Stoki.

"Oh yes there is," quickly retorted Stoki. "There is Maestro Morse."

"Maestro" Morse—twenty-two-year-old Tony Morse—was an assistant choral conductor at the St. Thomas School who had been hired to sort parts for Stoki and other conductors at the festival. Stoki was never at a loss, never at a loss.

The Morse suggestion cooled the atmosphere. After all, what could you say to *that?* There we stood: Red, Langton (he had sneaked in again), impresario Forest (he sneaked in with him), the head of the orchestra committee, a redheaded bass virtuoso named David Walter, and, of all people, the Hungarian fiddle-player of Stoki-Kandinski fame. Luckily that latter worthy shut up. We all did. Silence for at least two minutes. Then—abruptly—"Let's go back to work," from Stoki. And *l'affaire* Red Buttons was over.

The performance was good, but there was very little music: a few hundred harmless bars with which the unspeakable fascists were going to replace the superb musical fantasy-world which the Jew Felix Mendelssohn added to Shakespeare's.

♪

Stokowski has always been the quintessence of the glamorous conductor, and a principal reason for this was his reputation as a great lover. Going back to my student days, I remembered that it was his romantic forays that occasioned most of the talk about him.

I took fiddle lessons in a Rittenhouse Square studio, and the occupant of the apartment directly above was Philadelphia's *première* ballerina, making her somewhat less eminent than Pavlova, dance not being one of Philadelphia's strong points. My teacher, who lived in the studio, regaled his panting students with tales of Stokowski's late-evening visits to the lady, and of a record player sending the passionate measures of the *Tristan* love music flowing down through the whole apartment house. They seem to have liked it very loud. (The recording was, of course, the Stokowski arrangement, a dreadfully mutilated affair which would have stunned Wagner.) The most piquant part of the story was our teacher's smirking relation of how the last side of the album—it was in automatic sequence—would be repeated over and over far into the night. There seemed to be no one available to turn it off.

There was always an aura of sex around Stoki, though his first marriage was a fairly routine music-world match. He had married Olga Samaroff, an American piano virtuosa, in the early 1920s. (Her name reminded one of the Stokes-Stokowski affair, except that Olga really did have a problem. Her real name was Hickenlooper, and she could hardly be faulted for adopting another name—any other name. Samaroff sounded Russian or Polish, at a time when most name-pianists were either one or the other.) The marriage ended in divorce, and, whether there was any connection or not, Mme. Samaroff's career as a virtuosa faded.

Stoki's second marriage was to the affluent Evangeline Johnson, of the baby-powder company. They were divorced in the late 1930s and became good friends again in the early 1960s. I had the opportunity to meet the second Mrs. Stokowski at his apartment one day when he offered us tea—a unique occasion, because in all the hours I spent with him at home he never offered me anything but the hideously strong "Toork-ish" or "Bool-gahr-ian" cigarettes he liked. He smoked European style, cigarette held between thumb and middle finger, puckering his lips into a complete circle and looking distractingly like some remarkable specimen of marine life. At any rate, I got tea when I was there with Evangeline, who turned out to be handsome, a little loud, and full of minor reminiscences.

"Stoki" (she was the only one I ever heard call him Stoki to his face), she would begin, "do you remember that wonderful little restaurant in Brussels that you said had the best chocolate you had ever tasted?"

"No," answered Stoki.

Evangeline pressed on. "Stoki, do you remember that car we had built? I think it was a three-wheel job or something. Amazing!"

"No," answered Stoki.

Undeterred, Evangeline continued to reminisce. "Stoki, did we ever find out what happened to that marvelous young painter that did your portrait one Christmas? Handsome little devil," Evangeline guffawed. She was really a little loud.

Stoki muttered something. I took it to be a negative,

but I couldn't be sure it was anything.

"By the way, Stoki, do you have any other cigarettes around? These damn things are killing me. They're like cigars."

"No."

"Stoki, do you ever go to Mexico anymore? God, how I loved it. Remember that trip to Yucatan with the— what was their name?"

"No."

"Good God, Stoki, you are a fount of information." She didn't seem at all put out. In fact, she chuckled, almost as if his taciturnity were charming.

"Stoki, don't you have any cakes or anything to go with this awful tea? Mr. Toobin looks kind of skinny, and he'll starve to death with you for a host." Stoki said no. No cakes. No anything.

But the peak of the Stokowski romantic legend came with Greta Garbo. In the late thirties, the conductor and the fabulous actress began a relationship that culminated in a fairy-tale idyll on the Isle of Capri. Readers of the Philadelphia *Evening Bulletin* palpitated (in earlier times they would have swooned), nay trembled, as they read of the almost too-much-for-fiction story of the Great Lovers—peerless in their arts—doing whatever they were doing together. And—music up and over—on the Isle of Capri.

But, alas, it all came to naught. After that one magical (I suppose) summer, Stoki came back to Locust Street, and Garbo to MGM. And cynics say that it was by no means an affair to put alongside Tristan's or Romeo's or any of those star-crossed folks'. In fact, it is said that what brought Stoki and Greta to the Isle of Capri was passion—but passion for (I blush to report what I have been told by sources close to Stoki) the *healthy* life. Rosy cheeks and vigor and all that kind of salubrious stuff, don't you know. In short, the blond maestro and Camille were brought together by the health-food–physical-culture regimen that both adopted. Stoki was still standing on his head a lot in my days with him, and I had, as a boy, tried lichee nuts and dates because it was widely reported that Stoki was practically living on them. Remember that Garbo, after Stokowski, traveled with Gaylord Hauser. In short, Greta and L. S. were health nuts, and this drew them together. So they went all over Europe doing pre-breakfast calisthenics that would have made the Canadian Air Force blanch, and dining sumptuously on assorted nuts and berries. The assumption, sad to tell, is that it may have been an almost indecently licit affair. But no one will ever know, and the story certainly heated the staid old pages of the Philadelphia *Evening Bulletin* to the combustion point.

I was tempted—oh, how I was tempted—to ask Stoki about Garbo, but I never did. Once he alluded to her—at least I assume it was to her—when a willowy blonde who had worked for Dag Hammarskjöld applied for a job as the fluctuating secretary. She was very, very well favored. I was entranced, but Stoki was matter-of-fact.

"What are you?" he asked.

I didn't quite get that but she apparently did, because she answered, in a delightful, soft Scandinavian accent, "I am Swedish."

"Oh," said Stoki. "I once had a Swedish girl friend." And that was all. I *assume* it was Garbo.

Stoki never impressed me as a great connoisseur of women—he just seemed to like them all, provided they were not veritable beasts. One week, when the Sym-

phony of the Air was doing a series of midnight recordings—this was an hour when all the best personnel were
available—Stoki, Gunther Schuller, now a great panjan-
drum in American music, and then A & R man on the
sessions, and I would go out at 3:00 a.m. or so in search
of some refreshment. World metropolis though it is,
New York has very few places open at that hour—at
least any that are reasonably posh—and I did try to impress Stoki. So we went for five straight nights to Reubens, sandwich heaven of the stars. There, we would see
the late-blooming roses with their escorts, and Stoki
would almost fall out of the booth looking them over.

"There is a very attractive girl," he would say, referring, I'm afraid, to a floozyish ("hennaed" my mother
would call her) female who was old enough to remember Stoki's great days and was built like a linebacker.
No, he was pretty indiscriminate, I thought, at least in
his late seventies.

At Reubens, one morning just before dawn (we were
there usually till 5:00 a.m.), Stoki suddenly asked his two
startled companions, "Have either of you ever made
love to a lesbian?"

Our feeble retorts amounted to, "Not to the best of our
knowledge."

Stoki, as usual not waiting for an answer, continued:
"It's wahn-dah-fooll. They act—and they pretend—and
they try to—what you say—convince themselves. It's
wahn-dah-fooll. Oh, you should sometime. You will enjoy it."

What brought that on I'll never know, because the
ladies of the evening that kept coming in, even at this
near-breakfast hour, looked like many things, but not
lesbians. Still, something had impelled Stoki to make

that query, and it is among the unanswered questions I
have about my boyhood idol.

I've mentioned Stokowski's lack of undue reverence
for his contemporaries, but one contradiction comes to
mind. We got on the subject of Bernard Shaw once, lord
knows how, and Stoki told me he admired him a great
deal. "I once found myself in the same railroad coach
with Shaw, near London," Stokowski told me, "and I
wanted to approach him. But I knew I wouldn't be able
to talk to him about anything." I was about to remind
Stokowski that Shaw, as a retired music critic, might
have had things to talk to Stokowski about. But Stokowski quickly added, "But, you know, Shaw was lacking in
—in—how shall I say, *volupté*. He never knew what
women were for." Far more erudite scholars of the
Shavian canon took many more words, nay volumes, to
say the same thing.

(As to Shaw on Stokowski, I found an interview with
Shaw in the London *Times,* done in the early 40s, in
which he was prevailed on to comment on the musical
scene. After his great music-critic days as "Corno di
Bassetto," Shaw rarely talked music. But here he dis-
coursed on some current topics, and the interviewer
threw out the name Stokowski for evaluation. "Oh, the
cinema person!" Shaw responded. "I really don't know
much about him." This was after *One Hundred Men
and a Girl,* and *Fantasia,* and a few cameo appearances
by Stokowski in the "Big Broadcast" movies of the 30s.
I think Shaw was being nasty, a quite natural role.)

Immediately after the New York Coliseum opened,
Stokowski asked me to broach to its management the
idea of giving children's concerts there. They evinced

mild interest, and Stoki called me and said, "We must go there and make tests for acooostic!" Stoki loved to make tests for "acooostic" everywhere he went. No acoustical expert to start with, I was always baffled by his hand-clappings and hootings and echo-listenings. "Get, please, a trumpet and a drum and we will make tests at Coh-lee-say-ohm." "Trumpet" and "drum" meant trum-peter and drummer in orchestral parlance. I called Juilliard and told them we would pay some students of trumpet and drum to play notes for Stokowski, a double privilege, I thought. I asked the players to meet us at the hall at 7:00 p.m. on the designated date.

Stoki and I showed up to find that "trumpet" was a young lady of about twenty, average-looking—I can't picture her at all now. "Drum" was a lad about the same age. Stoki "made test," the kids played stray notes at his command, he clapped his hands, he hooted, he listened for echoes, and in about forty-five minutes we were through. "Thank you," said Stokowski. "Good night."

At 9:00 a.m. the next morning—I was always at my desk very early to see what disaster had struck during the night and what litigation the morning mail announced—the phone rang and it was Stokowski.

"Good morning. Who was trumpet?"

"Sir?"

"Come now, who was trumpet? Is she your mistress?"

For just a moment I took umbrage. "Trumpet" was a pretty ordinary-looking girl. But I rallied and ran true to life, Toobin vis-à-vis Stoki.

"No, Maestro, I never saw her before in my life."

"Ah, you should have. She's a very attractive girl. She looks passionate. You should get to know her."

"What did you think of her trumpet playing?" I asked.

"Terrible," he answered. "But she was lovely. Just lovely."

The "acooostics" were also terrible, he added. But since we were never asked to play in the Coliseum, there was no problem.

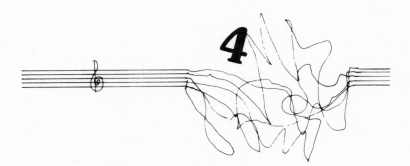

In February 1956 I was new on the job at the Symphony of the Air, but exhilarated by the prospect before us. The principal item of anticipation was a tour by the orchestra of the Near East, under the joint sponsorship of the State Department and the American National Theatre Academy (ANTA).

The previous spring, May and June 1955, a tour of the Far East had been an enormous success, the orchestra having played in Japan, the Philippines, Korea, Okinawa, Thailand, Formosa, Ceylon, and Malaya. The conductors for the trip were two good but not celebrated conductors, Thor Johnson and Walter Hendl. The tour had been scheduled rather hurriedly and no big-name maestros were available. The men all talked about their oriental odyssey as if it were some happy dream fulfilled. They were amazed by the rapturous welcomes they received everywhere, and overwhelmed that the fame of Toscanini's orchestra—for it was so billed and promoted in all the exotic locales they visited—was so great. Photographs they showed me corroborated their passionate accounts of lines forming twenty-four hours in advance of concerts, and looking for all the world like crowds gathering the night before the World Series. They talked about the wonders of Japan, which they all loved and vowed to revisit at the first opportunity. Incidentally, they raved about Japanese women to the point that *I* was vowing to revisit Japan, and I had never *been* there.

As a result of the smashing success of the Far East tour, the State Department and ANTA immediately began negotiations with the Symphony of the Air for another trip, this time to Turkey, Egypt, Israel, India, and some other locales to be arranged more or less at the last minute. When I joined the orchestra, first as public relations director, and a month later as administrative director (manager), the only thing lacking was a completed itinerary and a signed contract between the Symphony of the Air and the State Department–ANTA. The pressure for such a contract, from the men and the concert brokers, was enormous, since an engagement of three months was in prospect, plans had to be made, and a great deal of money was involved.

The head of ANTA at this time was Robert W. Dowling, Broadway producer, Democratic bigwig, and owner of the Hotel Carlyle, where so many presidential nights were passed. Much of the pressure on me I tried to share with Dowling, but Broadway-producer–Democratic-bigwig–hotel-owner types are difficult to reach, and I became a very good telephone friend of Dowling's secretary. One day, to my astonishment, Dowling called me and asked that I assemble the top officials of the orchestra and meet with him at the Oak Room of the Plaza at 5:00 p.m. that day. There was a matter-of-fact quality to his tone that soothed my usual raging anxieties, and I set up the meeting in a mood of contentment. We were about to sign the contract.

At 5:00 p.m. we presented ourselves at the Plaza's famous watering place. The group consisted of David Walter, a bassist, chairman of the board of the orchestra, and its chief executive; Arthur Granick, a master violist and a man of great sensitivity and culture, who was the treasurer; and a member of the board, Filippo Ghignatti, the English-horn player who had played under Toscanini as far back as the La Scala days of the 1920s. Dowling was waiting for us at a table.

"I'm having tomahto juice," were his first words. "What are you having? I'm having tomahto juice." Tomahto juice all around was in order.

"Gentlemen, that trip you were going on? Well, I'm afraid you're not going."

We said nothing as the drinks, such as they were, arrived. Dowling sipped, and I, suddenly parched, gulped tomato juice.

David Walter, a jovial-looking redhead, with a beaked nose that seemed incongruous in his pleasant face, spoke first. He was a very articulate, urbane man of about forty-five, who had joined Toscanini a year or so after Maestro came to the NBC.

"Well, Mr. Dowling, that *is* news. Whatever happened?"

Dowling, about six foot four, craggy-faced, aristocratic, towered over us it seemed even as we sat. He spoke as though none of this was of very great moment.

"I'm not very clear about what happened. All I know is that I got a call from Mr. McIlvaine at the State Department and he told me to call you fellows and tell you the trip was off. When I asked him why, he said, 'Better you shouldn't know.' So that's it."

Granick, who spoke very slowly and seemed at the best of times deeply melancholy, asked if there was any hope of discussing the matter further and salvaging the tour. Dowling began to seem just a trifle impatient and said no, he didn't think so, and we should begin to "rework our plans."

Ghignatti, a dignified, elderly, extremely handsome gentleman, said in his finely accented English, "This is not fair. We are being hurt very badly. And you say there is nothing to do. This is not fair." And he looked deeply hurt.

But Dowling continued to be very cool and said, "Well, that's it. We'll talk later about how the announcement will be made. Of the cancellation, that is. And now, if there is nothing else?"

Well, there was plenty else for these men, for Toscanini's orchestra, for music in America, for the arts in America, above all, for decency in the government's attitude toward the arts and people in general. But Dowling got up, his "tomahto" juice almost, but not quite, finished, and he shook hands all around, and left.

This was a Monday. By late Thursday I had found out the reason for the cancellation in a telephone call from a most surprising source. My secretary told me that Frederick Woltman of the *World-Telegram* was calling. I knew him to be a zealous Red-hunter whose stock in trade was digging up Communist affiliations for celebrities. Naturally his Red-hunting was no good if there wasn't publicity in it. So I was both apprehensive and baffled.

"Hi there," he greeted me in what sounded like great good humor. "What do you think of these Rooney hearings?"

Now I suspected mistaken identity—not uncommon

in the Red-hunting fraternity. "What Rooney hearings?"

"The ones on the Symphony of the Air. You mean you haven't been informed? Well, don't worry, it will be going out on the wire services tomorrow morning."

I liked that "don't worry."

"Can you tell me what this is all about?" I asked, not worried, just petrified.

"Well, Rooney—the Congressman from Brooklyn, you know—is holding closed sessions of his House Subcommittee and accusing the State Department of sending your orchestra to the Far East without investigating it carefully. And it turns out the orchestra's full of Communists. Also they have a lot of bad information on your conductor, Bernstein."

I interrupted. "Bernstein is *not* our conductor. He is doing some concerts with us, but he has no official position at all with us."

Leonard Bernstein was, indeed, conducting six Carnegie Hall concerts with the Symphony of the Air during this period and utilizing the orchestra in the first of his famous TV shows.

"I don't know about that," Woltman continued, "but my sources tell me that Bernstein is as much involved in this affair as the Symphony of the Air. By the way, they are using numbers instead of names for the principals in the hearings. Do you know why?"

"How do I know that when I don't even know there are any hearings?"

"Well, you better find out quick," he said, suddenly sounding testy. "This isn't going to do you any good." It didn't.

My first impulse, after Woltman hung up, was to see the funny side. The orchestra was about half veteran Toscanini men who had served NBC for an average of ten to twelve years, and the rest, fluctuating younger personnel. Woltman said it was "full of Communists." How could anybody make that out? There we were seeking desperately for the best available musicians in New York to augment men who had been hand-picked and approved by Toscanini, and some politician was seeing it as a Communist apparatus! I pictured our wildly individualistic, eccentric, self-centered players. Would they have gummed up a revolution! The only things—absolutely the *only* things—I ever heard more than three of them at a time agree on were that Toscanini was the greatest and that they weren't making enough money. Politics? Who ever talked politics when the griping about money, conductors, working conditions, the personnel manager, Toobin, took all the time at breaks and rehearsals, and post-concert *Kaffeklatschen*. All *I* could picture was the boys standing around in little knots and berating everything from the dragging tempo the latest maestro had found for the Brahms First, to Toobin's failures in getting the ten million dollars that would have assured the orchestra's future. Still, I didn't sleep well that Thursday night.

The next morning, the first call came. From Harold Schonberg of *The New York Times.* "What the hell is this stuff coming in on the wire about the Symphony? Something about Communists all over the place. I can't make head or tail of it." And lo and behold, the *Times* was a press-relations man's dream. We made the front page. Oh, did we ever make it! The headline on the story read: CHARGE OF RED TAINT BARS SYMPHONY TRIP.

I thought they could have phrased it somewhat better, though days later the *Times,* in a strong editorial, called for an end to the baiting of the orchestra and immediate reinstatement of the tour.

The transcript of the Hearings of the Committee on Appropriations, House of Representatives, makes for rueful reading. John Rooney, of Brooklyn, the Subcommittee chairman, on March 14, 1956, asked Robinson McIlvaine, deputy assistant secretary of state for public affairs (to whom Dowling told us he had spoken), "Last summer did you send an organization known as the Symphony of the Air to the Orient?" After some routine questions as to the number of men, the itinerary, and the cost to the taxpayers ($267,005.09), Rooney moved to the attack.

ROONEY: Before you sent these people, Mr. McIlvaine, at a cost of two hundred and sixty-seven thousand dollars to the taxpayers, did you have their names checked for security?

MCILVAINE: Yes, we did.

ROONEY: Who did you have check them?

MCILVAINE: We had the management and the conductors checked by the Department's Security Office.

ROONEY: I think from here on we should use numbers in referring to them.

Now some further excerpts from the testimony which convey, I think, the flavor, the level, the seriousness of what was, alas, in the post-McCarthy era, the 1956 of John Rooney and his ilk.

ROONEY: In this group that you sent to the Orient, known as the Symphony of the Air, were they all dependable

Americans without Communist connections?

MCILVAINE: I am not saying that; no sir. However, the Symphony of the Air was a great success, from the point of view of everything that we have heard of it.

Now the second criteria, in which you are interested, and in which I am interested, that all participants be good representatives of the United States, is much less susceptible to precise determination; clearly participants should not be persons who are Communists, or who might otherwise act against the interest of the United States. That includes various types, people who have nothing to do with communism, but who would be just plain poor representatives of the United States.

ROONEY: How about Communist sympathizers?

MCILVAINE: That could include those too.

ROONEY: It should, should it not?

MCILVAINE: Yes. Making a determination in the case of an individual is a very difficult thing. It is relatively easy with respect to stars and top performers, because they are frequently well known by reputation and otherwise. And of course, as you already know, we do submit their names for a name check.

The problem becomes much more difficult when you are dealing with a large group that operates as a team. Now a symphony is a good example of this. We are dealing with their reputation as an entity; and the top ones have international reputations as orchestras, because of the conductors and managers, and so on, who have been able to produce a team that produces music. The spotlight does not often get down to the third violin player, or other routine performers Nevertheless I think we do have to consider what kind of a person that third player of the violin is, and it is not very easy to determine. For example, we might get unverified information, concerning a hypothetical violin player, describing him as a left-winger or that he belongs to a do-good organization that was infiltrated with Communists, in the past.

Our security people tell me that you often will find quite a proportion of such people who have had such associations, in this field, and I believe that the people themselves admit that people in this area are somewhat naive about such political things as the Communist conspiracy. So we had to make an operating decision in this program. And our decision was that since the President and the Congress had determined that this program was in the national interest we must try to make it work. In doing so we recognized that we must take all practical precautions to insure the proper type of performers; that in the case of large groups it was impractical to scrutinize each individual performer and that, therefore, our trust must be put in the management and the principals with whom we constantly stress the role that they and all their group play as unofficial ambassadors.

Thus, as a practical matter our assumption was if the hypothetical third violin player is a good one the overall effect of his participation in a great orchestra will far outweigh any mischief he might be able to do in the relatively few hours he is left alone on one of these tours.

ROONEY: Suppose it was said, as was written to me in a letter, that during the visit of the above-named band last year to the Orient, a good number of the members were spreading Red propaganda in the nations and islands they visited; would you then say that the third violinist's ability would outweigh the mischief he might be able to do?

MCILVAINE: I would say that was bad; except for this one member that we know about, and I have no evidence that they did. However I agree that it certainly would be bad if they did. On the other hand we have had very very heavy evidence that the overall impact of the tour was highly successful.

ROONEY: Perhaps the music was better than the third violin player?

MCILVAINE: Undoubtedly it was. Most of the reports we have had in have specifically mentioned the favorable impression made by the individual performers.

I am not so naive as to believe, or to state to you that in no instance did a single American performer make a fool of himself in any of these countries, or for that matter did not talk against the interest of the United States. But I do believe that the evidence in our files shows that the overall impact of this program far outweighed any possible bad effect that was given by an individual.

Now let us go into the details of this particular orchestra. This tour was organized over a year ago, and we used the Symphony of the Air, first of all because it has· a reputation of being among the top in the country, and second because at the time it was thought best to send it, a number of the city name orchestras could not go; and in accordance with the policy we had adopted, we checked the president of the orchestra and the two conductors. . . .

One of the great Japanese newspapers put up a $74,000 guaranty for their appearance in Tokyo, and arrangements were made with the Defense Department for them to play for the troops in Okinawa, Korea, and Japan; and other arrangements were made for them to play throughout the Orient. The tour was not without its problems. We were really pioneering. This is the first time a symphony has ever gone to the Far East, and there were a great many problems involving such things as booking arrangements, transportation, and so forth.

The report from Japan was extravagant, but typical of what we received from all the stops. It was described as the greatest cultural event that has happened in Japan since the opening of that country to the Western World.

Just last month the leading Philippine university cited the visit of the Symphony of the Air as the outstanding cultural event of the year, and presented Ambassador Ferguson with a citation to this effect for transmittal to the orchestra. . . .

At one stage of the tour the orchestra was traveling in planes chartered from General Chennault's CAT airline. So pleased were the members of the orchestra with the friendly and efficient manner the pilots and crew handled the operation that they took up a collection for them. The pilots said they could not accept such a gift but would turn it over to the Formosa Symphony which was having a difficult time.

A recent letter from Taipei informs that this contribution has given the Formosa Symphony a new lease on life and that they look on the Symphony of the Air as their cultural godparents.

The comments from the other places were in the same vein. Everywhere they went tribute was paid to the excellence of the performance and the impressions of the performers as individuals.

On the basis of their record we considered the Symphony of the Air for another tour next year, but something happened. . . .

ROONEY: Who was the conductor of the orchestra at that time?

MCILVAINE: There was no conductor as yet.

FLINN: That is correct.

MCILVAINE: This orchestra does not have a regular conductor; they get people to be guest conductors. I feel that—

ROONEY: Is No. 5 one of the conductors of this orchestra?

MCILVAINE: He has been a guest at various times. At the present time he would not be on any of our programs.

ROONEY: Has he been associated with the orchestra within the past year?

MCILVAINE: I believe he has, when it plays in the United States. . . .

Then, when Mr. McIlvaine was finished, Rooney called on Dennis A. Flinn, a State Department security officer (who had interjected the few words above).

ROONEY: On or about the 18th of January 1956 were you in touch with me, Mr. Flinn?

FLINN: That is correct.

ROONEY: At that time I told you that I had the name of a certain person in the city of New York which had been sent to me by a retired detective of the police department of that city?

FLINN: That is correct.

ROONEY: And did I give you a copy of the letter?

FLINN: You gave me a copy of the portion of the letter without the signature of your correspondent.

ROONEY: But including the name and address and telephone number of the informant?

FLINN: That is correct.

ROONEY: And what did you then do?

FLINN: I referred this—since the information contained in the letter appeared to come within the internal security jurisdiction of the FBI, I referred it to the FBI.

ROONEY: What did you then find?

FLINN: The FBI made the investigation and submitted the results to the State Department.

ROONEY: And what did it report?

FLINN: They reported the interview with the original informant named in the letter to you, sir, and the results of the names-check of those persons he named including others in this orchestra who had gone on this Far East tour.

ROONEY: Let us stay with the original informant—the first person they interviewed.

FLINN: Yes, sir.

ROONEY: We will call him No. 6.

FLINN: Yes.

ROONEY: What did No. 6 say?

FLINN: He identified himself as associated with this orchestra in the past, and stated that since the election of officers of the orchestra, when the leftist group took control, he has not played with the orchestra.

ROONEY: Excuse me a moment.

FLINN: Certainly.

ROONEY: Very well, proceed. We were inquiring with reference to what No. 6 said.

FLINN: He attributed his lack of further employment with the orchestra to an incident that took place in 1955 when the arrangements were made for the trip to the Orient, which the orchestra made. He had made a comment to one of the members of the orchestra that some of the fellows were going to have difficulty—

ROONEY: He made the comment to No. 7; and who was No. 7?

FLINN: I do not have that—he is a member of the symphony.

ROONEY: The manager of the orchestra?

FLINN: Apparently that has certain information better than I have on this paper.

ROONEY: Are you looking at the report of February 15?

FLINN: No, I am looking at the raw material which I received, and I have identified the man there, but I did not identify him here, you see.

ROONEY: Very well.

FLINN: He said that he had made this comment to No. 7 that some of the fellows were going to have difficulty in making the tour because they would have difficulty in getting a passport.

ROONEY: Did he say, because of their background?

FLINN: Because of their background. No. 7 replied that if he continued to talk in this manner that he would never play with the orchestra again.

Since that statement No. 6 said that he was constantly watched by the "leftists," while in the Far East. He also described an incident which occurred while on the tour, where he was given a "trial," when he was charged by other members of the orchestra with using vile language in the presence of an Army officer's wife. This trial resulted in proof that No. 6 did not make these comments in front of—in the presence of ladies, and it seems as though—and I am interpolating now, that in some of the comments made by No. 6 there is a showing of spite. However, he did name approximately 30 people associated with the orchestra, which he identified as the "leftist" group.

ROONEY: Was No. 6 asked to elaborate on his allegation that some of the Symphony of the Air members spread "red" propaganda while on the tour of the Orient?

FLINN: Yes.

ROONEY: What did he say?

FLINN: He stated that No.——

ROONEY: That is No. 8?

FLINN: I will leave out the designation, because that identifies him. That No. 8 had highly praised and agreed with the book which contained . . . He said this, that No. 8 highly praised and agreed with a book which condemned the atom bombing of Hiroshima. Another example of propaganda given by the informant was the fact that number—

ROONEY: That is what number?

FLINN: No. 9, associated with the orchestra, constantly praised Russian music and stated that its culture was superior to ours. He added that while at army installations in the Far East, the musicians with the orchestra took photographs. He admitted that he could not be specific as to the allegations of the red propaganda, nor cite specific instances as to the spread of that propaganda. He did furnish, however, a list of 30 individuals suspected by him of being "leftists."

This informant was also not quite articulate when asked to define the term "leftist."

ROONEY: Did he not say that he believed there were certain people who were un-American?

FLINN: Un-American; yes.

And so it went—and I believe it is sufficient unto itself to establish the nature of Rooney's attack on the Symphony of the Air.

It is interesting to note that throughout the testimony Rooney was trying to embarrass the State Department, whose chief was then John Foster Dulles, for having sent a Communist-infested orchestra to the Orient, "at an expense to the taxpayers of $267,000": even that crusty old warrior in the anti-Communist crusade was subjected to the charge of abetting the Devil's cause, if only by the laxity of his subordinates. I have found no record of what Mr. Dulles thought about the Symphony of the Air.

While the Rooney hearings may have had comic overtones, there was really nothing funny about them to the Symphony of the Air and its future. As a matter of fact, although the Symphony did not fail until 1963, it never fully recovered from the shock of the Rooney attack. When the hearings came, we were about to embark on another extensive tour, the publicity attendant to it was opening many avenues of revenue, and it looked as if the improbable might happen, and the orchestra survive the severance from NBC. But the cancellation, the bad publicity, the uncertainty about our ability to survive were the beginning, however protracted, of the end.

Much has been conjectured regarding what really happened in 1954 when the orchestra was dissolved by NBC after Toscanini's retirement. I am relying chiefly on second-hand information in my own account, but one of my sources was a most reliable one. I am referring to the brilliant young conductor Guido Cantelli, who died in an air crash late in 1956 while returning to New York from Italy to conduct the New York Philharmonic.

Before I met Cantelli, the orchestra men, incensed at NBC for withdrawing its support, were full of horror stories about the callous attitude of the network toward them, and particularly toward their efforts to keep the orchestra alive after NBC's action. Toscanini's last season ended April 4, 1954, and a day or so later the orchestra men got six weeks' notice, and that was to be that. Efforts to keep the orchestra going without NBC began almost immediately, spearheaded by Don Gillis, who had been the producer of the Symphony broadcasts, and by a group of orchestra players.

In May 1954 an orchestra committee set an appointment with Samuel Chotzinoff, the NBC executive responsible for the orchestra's administration and the man who had gone to Italy in 1937 to negotiate with Toscanini his agreement to become music director of an NBC Symphony Orchestra, formed especially for the Maestro. The orchestra committee reported a short, unfriendly meeting with Chotzinoff. After they had given their exposition of why they felt the orchestra should survive even its great conductor, that it had for seventeen years brought glory and honor to RCA and was conceded to be one of the most important orchestras in American musical history, they concluded, feelingly they thought, on the note that the symphony's existence would be the most significant living tribute to Toscanini.

Chotzinoff listened and, when they were through, said, "Do you really want to honor Toscanini? Then die." A pause. "Your orchestra, I mean," he concluded, lamely. "Then die" became a rallying cry around orchestral headquarters for years.

After I became manager of the Symphony of the Air, I had a similar encounter with Chotzinoff. After Cantelli was killed, I went to Chotzinoff and asked if NBC would carry on radio, and perhaps on TV, a memorial concert for Cantelli with some eminent conductors sharing the podium. I began with a lengthy, and *I* thought touching, description of what Cantelli had meant to the Maestro and to the men, and what a searing tragedy his untimely death was. Left unsaid, however, was the well-known fact that Toscanini had hoped that Cantelli would succeed him as conductor of the Symphony, given there was a Symphony. I tried very hard and undoubtedly talked too long. Chotzinoff sat stolidly before me, a stocky, neckless man who always wore a black suit and a black bow tie. I finished.

"Well," he said, apparently having heard nothing I had said, "what do you want from us?"

I repeated the request for a memorial concert, as well as I could in the frigid atmosphere.

"No," said Chotzinoff. "Next question."

I had none.

The orchestra committee's report on the adamant refusal of NBC to help them stay alive corroborated, to some extent, Cantelli's account of what happened in 1954. Cantelli, who visited Toscanini almost daily in Riverdale whenever he was in New York, and was as close to being a protégé of the Maestro as any musician ever was, told me that early in 1953, when plans were being drawn up for the 1953–1954 season, NBC informed Toscanini, through his son, Walter, that 1953–1954 was to be the last year of the orchestra's existence. Walter reported this to his father, who was not pleased at the report. To be sure, the Maestro was almost eighty-seven, but he was in the same condition he had been in for the last five years or so, when the NBC Symphony concerts had been uniformly superb. (It must not be forgotten that RCA netted many millions from Toscanini-record sales.) Certainly Toscanini was near the end of his fabulous career, but Cantelli felt that he should have been allowed the prerogative of deciding when he would lay down his baton. At any rate, Toscanini was furious with Chotzinoff and his superiors at RCA, and always referred to them in his conversations with Cantelli as the *animali.* His famous "Dear David" letter of resignation (to David Sarnoff) sat on Toscanini's desk for months before he would sign it.

Cantelli was an extremely sensitive, serious, handsome man in his thirties at this time. He was short, wiry, nervous, and spoke a lovely broken English. Toscanini had brought him to New York after hearing him conduct in Italy. Maestro told the critic B. H. Haggin, the outstanding Toscanini authority of our time, "I love this young conductor. I think is like me when I was young."

High-strung and emotional, Cantelli had been engaged by practically all of the major orchestras in America as a guest, including the New York Philharmonic, but his association there was not a happy one. Accidentally, I was with Cantelli when that unfortunate situation reached a climax.

Cantelli was very lonely in New York, having no taste for socializing or New York's high life, and except for his constant visits with Toscanini, he stayed most of the time in his Essex House suite (very small) and studied scores. I had interviewed him on radio in 1955, while I was still working in Philadelphia, and we became friends. We talked a great deal about the future of the Symphony of the Air, and I made no secret of my hopes that he would become its principal conductor when we could finance a proper season and pay him what he needed. He made his interest clear, though he seemed to hint at divisions within the Toscanini family itself in attitudes toward the Symphony after the Maestro stepped down. While Maestro still talked to him about the orchestra, certain players, and his desire to conduct again before he died, his children (Walter, Wanda Horowitz, the pianist's wife, and the Countess Castelbarco, who lived in Rome) seemed apathetic about the orchestra's existence. The Cantelli–Symphony of the Air association was a pet dream of mine, and like most dreams difficult to achieve. The fault was not in our stars, it was in our minuscule bank account.

So Cantelli was conducting the Philharmonic and loathing it. His chief interest at the time was a short season he was giving at the Piccola Scala in Milan (he had led a triumphant *Così fan tutte* before coming to New York that winter of 1955), and he was eager to talk about that and to try to forget the current engagement. One day we were to have lunch in his rooms after he returned from the Philharmonic rehearsal, where the soloist was the venerable Wilhelm Backhaus. Cantelli left word that if I got there before his return I was to be admitted to wait for him. I was looking at his score of *Così* when the door opened, and he walked in, looking desperate.

He ripped off his topcoat, threw it across the room, and shouted, "What 'oomiliation, such—such—such 'oomiliation. It is too much. I cannot stand this. I tell you, I can't stand this." And he sat down and buried his head in his hands. I said something about taking it easy or relaxing or something, but he was past simple ministrations.

"These men. They do not like me—good. I am not to like, you know. Nobawdy [Toscanini also said nobawdy and everybawdy] likes me. I am not to like. But to sit before a great artist like Backhaus and scratch at the strings, no vibrato, no feeling, just like this." And he raised an imaginary violin and imitated the playing of the first measures of the fourth Beethoven concerto—right after the piano's unaccompanied opening—conveying uninterested, bland, dead, dull playing. "No, it is too much. And Backhaus knew. He knew. Everyone knew. It was terrible. Terrible. I cannot do this. It is too much." And there—right there—Cantelli resolved to call Bruno Zirato.

Zirato was the manager of the Philharmonic, whose chief claim to fame was that he had been Caruso's secretary. He is a huge, burly man, gruff in manner, and not famous for kindness. Cantelli had been engaged to do a series of concerts with the Philharmonic the next fall, and he now resolved to call Zirato and ask to get out of the fall concerts on the basis of his work at the Scala and the fact that his wife was expecting a child around that time. But of course a major reason was his complete lack of rapport with the Philharmonic personnel, a notoriously tough, blasé, and jaded group. In front of me Cantelli placed the call to Zirato, spoke to him first calmly, then excitedly, then angrily in Italian, and though my Italian is primitive, the conversation was not hard to follow. He was being turned down, and his resigned, embittered tone toward the end indicated there was no hope of appeal. He put the phone down and looked at me, tears bright in his eyes. "He says no. He says I am too senseteeve. He says I am not strong. He says—he says no, and he will not listen to me."

Cantelli, unhappily resigned to live up to the contract, went back to Italy. That spring he flew from Milan to Paris, on his way back to New York, and was killed in a crash near the airport. This supremely gifted, honest, rigidly serious, probably unworldly young man was my friend, and I treasure that friendship. And it was Guido Cantelli who was my chief tie with Arturo Toscanini.

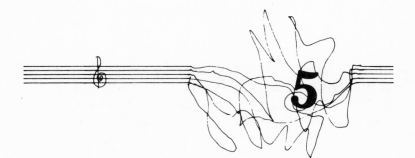

All during my first months with the Symphony, the name of Leonard Bernstein dominated the scene. Bernstein had been engaged to conduct six Carnegie Hall concerts with the Symphony of the Air in the 1955–1956 season. Given the precarious state of the Symphony's finances and its highly doubtful future, which existed even before the Rooney affair, it was remarkable that a never-ending procession of conductors, important and trivial, came to the orchestra with elaborate plans for huge financing if only that particular conductor were installed as music director.

Before my time the orchestra had benefited by about thirty thousand dollars when Kirsten Flagstad agreed to make two "comeback" appearances with the Symphony of the Air, both of which played to standing-room audiences. The mover of these concerts was Mme. Flagstad's accompanist and friend, Edwin MacArthur, an honorable man, who was not of the stature, however, to take over directorship of the Symphony of the Air only a year after Toscanini's departure. Still, certain men in the orchestra, careless rather than deceitful, and desperately hungry for the prestige and revenue of a Flagstad association, led MacArthur to believe that if he could prevail on the soprano to do the concerts, he would get the director's post. I have no doubt that Flagstad, always devoted to MacArthur and especially grateful to him for his staunch support during her post-war troubles, went out of her way to help him. MacArthur's contacts inside the orchestra later denied that any deal had been made, and it all ended in recrimination and bad feeling. I think it was greedy amateurism rather than evil intent, but it was grossly unfair to MacArthur and to the overwhelming majority of the orchestra which knew nothing of the manipulations.

(The management of the orchestra was in the hands of a nine-man board, elected from the ranks; it held sway until I became administrative director in late 1955, when we shared the responsibility. But despite the ruling body, the democratic nature of the symphony made every man a potential spokesman, and there were always one or two operators going their own way and purporting to speak for the group.)

Bernstein, however, was a logical candidate for the music director's post. He was young, famous, versatile, well connected, experienced. Perhaps the men in the orchestra were not fond of his flamboyant style, and the prospect of Bernstein as conductor was a very controversial subject. But Bernstein had no regular post then and was definitely interested in the Symphony of the Air. He evidenced this by engaging it for his very first "Omnibus" telecast, a program devoted to his analysis of the Beethoven Fifth Symphony. The orchestra, thrilled at the income and aware of Bernstein's rising star, decided on its first regular season in New York, with the same concerts being repeated in Newark. Bernstein chose six ambitious, very expensive concerts (though his own fee was very low), including a Mahler

Second, Stravinsky's *Oedipus Rex* (with Alistair Cooke
as narrator), the third act of *Manon Lescaut* with
Tebaldi and Jussi Bjoerling, and the *première* of a new
Bernstein work, featuring a famous violinist. The costs
being high, Bernstein not yet the draw he is today, and
the promotion spotty, the concerts were a financial
disaster, and the debts incurred were the beginning of
the deficit financing that prevailed throughout the pov-
erty-program life of the orchestra. Still, Bernstein had
to be considered for the future, even though many of the
players were strongly opposed to him.

I became manager of the Symphony in the middle of
the Bernstein series and was immediately put in the
position of buffer between conductor and orchestra. The
very first time I went up to Bernstein's apartment in the
famous old Osborne, across the street from Carnegie
Hall, I was in the middle of a hassle. *The New York
Time*'s Meyer Berger, who did excellent background
pieces about varied aspects of the city's day-to-day life,
wrote about a typical meeting of the Symphony of the
Air's orchestra board, and how it dealt with administer-
ing the orchestra. In this article Berger described the
board reviewing a program Bernstein had submitted for
one of his series of six. One board member, noticing a
Bernstein suggestion for some Vivaldi, demurred.

"Vivaldi? Lennie can't do Vivaldi. We better talk to
him about that."

There seems to have been agreement among the
board that Bernstein was not the man for baroque.
Berger gave the feeling of the meeting, a very informal
one, by stating that some of the men had their feet up
on a table (a huge rectangular one donated to the Symphony by a furniture dealer).

After greeting me cordially for about thirty seconds, Bernstein asked what I thought of the Berger piece, which I hadn't given much thought to. "I hope to hell," said Bernstein, "you can control those guys, with their goddamn feet up on the table saying, 'Lennie can't do Vivaldi.' Wow!" And he shook his head and looked at me pityingly. "You've got some job."

There was always friction of some kind or other about the rather overfamiliar way the orchestra treated Bernstein, but throughout his early career it was felt that he might have fostered this by the fact that he was "Lennie" to everyone, and would do things like run auditions while wearing riding boots and carrying a riding crop. (This was when he was conducting, at the City Center, the New York Symphony, which both he and Stokowski had directed with success.) But every once in a while he would object to the "Lennie" business, deeply ingrained though it was.

On one occasion, a group of orchestra players appeared on a late-night radio show to promote one of Bernstein's concerts. The next morning Bernstein's never-resting, passionately protective secretary, Helen Coates, called to protest in her best Down-East manner (she was the quintessential New England schoolmarm) at the way the musicians had referred to Bernstein as "Lennie" throughout the program. "My gracious. He's an important conductor and they talk about him as if he were some pop band leader. Can't you do anything? Gracious."

Miss Coates had been Bernstein's piano teacher in his Boston youth, and he had hired her as his secretary early in his rise. It was a brilliant move, for she was his sword and his buckler; she was the dragon in front of the castle that protected the king from all the world. New York—indeed the country—must be filled with poor souls who have had the temerity to try to reach Leonard Bernstein on some matter, sacred or profane, and who have come up against the immovable Helen Coates. Her hemmings, her hawings, her clipped Boston locutions have deterred a whole generation of Bernstein-seekers from their goal. You had better be pretty "in," or have some project of enormous portent if you expect to get through via Helen Coates. In my day, that was the *only* way.

But I got through all right. Too often. Once the board decided to do some business with Leon Barzin, a knowledgeable, eccentric conductor with whom many of the musicians had worked as students, since he was director of the National Orchestral Association, a famous New York training orchestra. Barzin was also conductor of the New York Ballet orchestra, and thus offered relatively steady employment. He was, for crescendo effect, married to the daughter of Mrs. Merriweather Post (of Toasties fame) and thus offered, some hoped, largess. The board decided to appoint Barzin musical adviser, whatever that meant, and not telling Bernstein anything about it, sent *The New York Times* a release announcing this nebulous appointment. Having been sent out a week before my arrival on the job, it appeared the day of my *second* visit to Bernstein in his apartment. The *Times* story, short though it was, did indicate that Barzin would be a power, even though *he* was conducting nothing with the orchestra, and Bernstein was for all intents and purposes its principal leader.

Bernstein greeted me with, "Well, your boys have done it again. What is it? Do they hate me so much?

Christ! They must hate me." Bernstein was understandably angry, and he walked around the room saying
"hate me" about five times. (He said "hayyyt," lingering
on the "ay" part longer each time until I thought it a
petulant rather than a violent anger.) "What the hell are
they doing with Leon Barzin? He won't give them a
dime. But it is so damned embarrassing to me. It's like
reading in the paper that your wife had a baby. I should
really get out, I really should. They really hayyyt me."
And he stroked his throat over and over, a mannerism
I was to become very acquainted with.

Well they didn't like him much, but they didn't hate
him that much either. They only thought that Barzin
might bring some sweet influences to bear on the Post
Toasties heiress, and Lord knows the need was there, for
every hour saw financial disaster move closer. Still, the
Barzin thing was badly handled, and Bernstein was
properly incensed. Of course Barzin never gave the orchestra anything but lots of advice.

A few weeks after I started working with Bernstein
came the Rooney affair, and it made him understandably jittery. Bernstein knew almost at once, through
friends inside and outside the orchestra, that his name
was being bandied about. He talked to me continually
on the phone, and Helen Coates talked to me, clucking
about how terrible this all was for "that poor boy." She
seemed to use up all her sympathy in that direction, for
never once did I hear her (or him) commiserate over
"that poor orchestra" or those other "poor boys." But
that was understandable, I guess. In fact, many people
were concerned about what the affair would do to them
personally.

A famous violinist, who was to appear as soloist with

the orchestra in its next concerts under Bernstein, called me from the coast and said, tremulously, "Jerry, what am I going to do? I'm supposed to go to Russia this spring and I have to play with you people." I was astonished, but, as so often, amused, because even as he whined on, I pictured conspiratorial rehearsals with the violinist utilizing every break to glean political information of momentous import to take to the USSR with him. But he went on: "Maybe you can get somebody else. Lennie will understand." Well, when I told Bernstein, he didn't understand at all and, though they were close friends, described the violinist in less than glowing terms. And the violinist did appear. (I had, to be sure, refused his request to "get somebody else.") But even the violinist's conduct was understandable. It was early 1956 and political fear and hysteria were common. These were nonpolitical or apolitical people, in the main, and they *did* live by their music, in every sense.

When I got the transcript of the hearings a week or so after the first disclosures, Bernstein asked to see a copy right away, and I brought one up to the Osborne at nine o'clock of a Saturday morning. Bernstein suffered from insomnia and usually didn't start working until around noon, but this was a special occasion. (His insomnia, indeed, made him the only one I knew who saw the "Late, Late, Late" show almost every night, and he often berated me for missing some great Marx Brothers film because I was "always sleeping.") Bernstein had with him his lawyer and adviser, Abe Friedman, an elderly man who looked like the stereotype of the lovable family doctor and had a manner to match. I can never forget Friedman's superb ability for keeping Bernstein and me from chattering too much about the unfortunate personalities and limited intellects of many of the protagonists in the Rooney affair. He was calm and worldly and good-humored and sagacious, and I have often wished I knew him better. Bernstein, a lucky man in general, was certainly lucky to have Abe Friedman.

Bernstein was very upset. A couple of weeks before he had startled me by asking, "Hey, do you know any spic talk?" This was his "in" way of describing Puerto Rican English, and I knew that he didn't mean it the way it sounded. When I told him I didn't know "spic talk," he informed me for the first time that he was finishing work on a new musical dealing with Puerto Ricans in New York. This was my introduction to *West Side Story*. I was amazed at his protean energy. Now, at the beginning of the meeting about the Rooney affair, he brought up his new show again. He literally clutched at his throat when he talked, and shook his head from side to side, and groaned. "My God, what a time for this. What a time. The show is almost ready and now this. Oh. What are we going to do, it's so—so—stupid, for Christ sake." And he wrung his hands, and chain smoked, and thrashed around. And he stroked his throat. Much of the time he lay on a sofa. He'd sit up, but only briefly, and lie down again.

And Friedman said, "Now take it easy, let's look at the stuff and see what it's all about. You know how ridiculous this stuff usually is."

And Helen said, "Now Lennie, stop taking on so. Gracious. It's all foolishness. Stop taking on so. Goodness."

And I sat there and agreed with everybody.

We began going through the material on number five, who it was agreed by all was Bernstein. Bernstein didn't remember half the organizations he was supposed to have joined and had never heard of the other half. He admitted in a calmer moment, with a giggle, that in his extreme youth he would join anything if they would put his name in print—Committees for Greek, Polynesian, Eskimo, or Transylvanian Freedom. He remembered letterheads, he told us, that read: "Agranapos, Avanopoulos, Bajoulopoulos, Bernstein, Cachamapoulos. . . ." No idea what the outfit really did, but he was a joiner if his name got in print. And he was twenty-two, twenty-three. During the war, when everybody joined everything. This was the grist for Rooney's mill. So Bernstein alternated between angry contempt and hysteria, Friedman soothing, Helen "my graciousing," Toobin sitting there.

Suddenly Friedman stopped and looked angry for the first time. "Hey, Lennie. It's one o'clock. We've been here four hours and you never even asked this guy [motioning to me] if he wants a glass of water. Or me either for that matter."

Bernstein sat upright on his sofa, and cried, "Oh, my God. I'm sorry. I'm sorry. Jerry, what do you want? Oh I'm sorry." He grabbed for my hand.

Helen, not overly moved by our deprivation, said, "Well, let's finish. Lennie is probably exhausted."

Friedman looked at her, and looked back at the transcript. He said he would get a copy from Washington and talk to me further. He never did. We adjourned soon after, Bernstein stroking my back as I stood in the doorway and saying, "No need to tell you how I feel about how you've been. You know. You know." And he stroked my back, and I left.

Throughout the meeting, I had thought how different Bernstein was from the almost frighteningly assured man I knew from television and podium speeches. Of course this investigation was very nerve-racking stuff. Still the contrast between the self-contained Bernstein I knew in Carnegie Hall and the writhing, throat-clutching man on the sofa before me was startling.

Actually this was practically the last time I saw Bernstein for any extended period, and certainly the last time we discussed the political affair. The series with Bernstein ended shortly thereafter, and there was no inclination on the part of Bernstein or the orchestra to renew the association. I did see Bernstein occasionally, but I didn't discuss the Symphony of the Air with him, and he didn't ask. I never found out how he avoided any public discomfiture over the Rooney affair.

An ironic note: when Bernstein was made music director of the Philharmonic in 1958, the *World-Telegram*, in an editorial, cheered the appointment as a great thing for American music, for America in general. As I read it, I thought of Woltman of the *World-Telegram* and his earlier comments on "your conductor, Bernstein."

The coda of my relationship with Leonard Bernstein had some strange notes. After his association with the Symphony of the Air ended, in the bizarre State Department debacle, I saw nothing at all of him, even though my office in the Carnegie Hall building and his home in the Osborne were diagonally across the street from each other. In 1958 Bernstein's career as a conductor reached its apex with his appointment to the music directorship of the New York Philharmonic, succeeding Dimitri Mitropoulos. This was only two years after the thoughts about Bernstein's being the saviour of the Symphony of the Air. When I first came to New York and was being a buffeted intermediary between Bernstein and the orchestra, he was full of ideas, some good, some revoltingly show-biz, about making the Symphony of the Air New York's "second orchestra"; in short, they were typically Bernstein. In one discussion, Bernstein assured me that he didn't need the Symphony of the Air assignment because he had been sounded out about many major musical posts, and of course he was at that time deeply involved with the musical theater. He told me about one opportunity, and frankly, I was very dubious about its authenticity.

"You know," he informed me, "I can have the Philharmonic any time I want to. Judson [Arthur Judson, at that time in his waning days as a colossal musical influence, was no longer manager of the Philharmonic, but most people close to the scene said that he was the most eminent *éminence grise* in musical history] told some friends of mine that it was time for the Philharmonic to get a Jew there as conductor so that it can get out of the doldrums it was in. The old bastard said that he doesn't like me much, but that I was the only guy around that fitted the bill." And L.B. laughed, with great contentment. And I, frankly, didn't believe him because I had heard that Judson hated him, and that he wasn't going to get anything from the Philharmonic. Another in my long, distinguished list of incorrect prognostications.

Bernstein, even though almost a decade had passed, was still smarting from the refusal of the Boston Symphony directors to heed what was practically Koussevitzky's death-bed wish to make Bernstein conductor of the BSO. In fact, there were two bitter footnotes to that history. One was that the BSO trustees, Cabots and their ilk, had decided against Bernstein for precisely the reason that Judson had opted for him: they didn't think the time was ripe for a Jew as music director of their group. The second footnote concerned Koussevitzky's successor. The story in Boston was that the revered Koussevitzky was incensed by the rejection of his beloved "Lenyushka," and when it was obvious that L.B. was out of the picture, Koussy turned almost cynical and suggested a musician that he had often been wryly critical of, the serviceable, but far from inspired, Charles Munch. Certainly there was nothing in Munch's past history (he was known chiefly as the accompanist on records for some French notables) to explain his appointment to what is one of the half-dozen most prestigious and powerful posts in the musical world.

So Bernstein was right, and he indeed did "get" the Philharmonic, and I wasn't seeing him much. Then one day I was over at the Osborne trying, as I remember, to keep some manager or other from suing us for the fee of some singer or other, when, lo, in the lobby, accoutered in riding clothes and clutching a riding crop, there he was. Greetings were warm, I congratulated him on his new post, I assured him how normal—that is, how terrible—things were at the Symphony of the Air, and when he asked me, solicitously, how long I was going to continue the ferocious, and inevitably doomed, battle to keep the Symphony of the Air alive, I said I wished to hell that I could just for a brief period work somewhere where every day might not be my last, both professionally and actually. "Why don't you come over and see me some afternoon?" he asked, and I said I sure would, thinking "how about in five minutes?"

But it was closer to a month later that I finally got past Miss Coates and saw the new music director of the Philharmonic in his apartment.

The manager of the New York Philharmonic at this time, but on the point of retirement, was Bruno Zirato. His successor was rumored to be the young George Judd, of an old, respected management family, his father George, Sr., having managed the Boston. Well, as Papageno sings, *"Wer viel wagt, gewinnt oft viel!"* (translated in most *Magic Flute* librettos meaningfully if inaccurately as "Nothing ventured, nothing gained"), I plunged right in, told L. B. I would love to work for the Philharmonic, and what's more, I thought I was qualified, and could do a good job as the manager. L. B. was sitting on a divan, in front of a table with what looked like hundreds of books and magazines on it, and the strange way the memory works, I can still remember, after these fifteen years or so, that the only opened book was a novel by Frederick Buechner.

Lennie had dragged into the room, his jacket over his shoulders in the familiar Bernstein manner, and was looking absolutely like death. I, to this day, have never seen anyone look as tired, as near sheer, total exhaustion as L. B. did after a work binge, and he did work absolutely fantastic hours at the multiplicity of his musical chores. He would come into a room with all the snap and briskness of Frankenstein's monster perambulating wherever he perambulated. And he slumped down, and said, exhaling, "Jesus, am I tired. I can't keep up this way. Jesus."

It was in this state that L. B. heard my job application. "Manager, huh. That's very provocative. Very provocative. You're damned good, you know."

I knew.

"Manager."

And he looked off into space. This was his "man-of-destiny" look. He adopted it a lot, his lips pursed as he seemingly looked at a prospect visible only to him.

"Manager. Yes, but what do you think about a Jewish manager and a Jewish conductor?"

Helen Coates had slipped into the room, and even though I was anything but pleased by her treatment of me during the political storm that boiled around L. B. and the Symphony of the Air, I liked her and knew that she basically liked me and was a friend in court. I thought her protectiveness of Lennie ranged from the absurd to the maniacal, and that she felt he was the First Coming—the Nazarene wasn't in it as compared with the kid from Brookline. But I was glad when I saw her enter the room, and she even blew me a kiss.

And when she heard L. B. ask his Jewish manager-conductor question, she burst out, uncharacteristically where her one-time piano student was concerned: "Land sakes, Lennie. [I swear, Helen Coates used to say, "Land sakes"] I think that's ridiculous. I don't think anybody would think a damn thing about it. [Incongruously, Helen swore a lot.] Good grief,who thinks about that kind of stuff any more?"

Lennie looked away from the private world he was scanning, first at Helen, then at me, and staggered to his feet, moaning a little. (Yes, I know, I'm talking about Leonard Bernstein that conducts as if he's fighting off a swarm of bees. But you ought to have seen him around the house when I used to.)

I agreed with Helen. What I thought about a Jewish manager and a Jewish conductor, in New York, circa 1958, was nothing. Zero.

But L. B. pursued his point.

And after he had risen, he changed from the "man of destiny" to the patient Father.

"Wait a minute. Wayy-t a minute [A great retard on the last wait a minute.] Calm down. Listen." All delivered with a combination of lordliness and condescension. If he hadn't looked so beat, I would have imagined the pose he was assuming was that of a Blakeian Yahweh, talking down to the Children of Israel. So he looked like a beat Yahweh talking down to an audience half of which was from among the Children of Israel.

"J. T., did you see my children's concert last week on TV? Anyway, at one point I was talking about nationalities, and I said that Mr. A. was Italian and Mr. B was Russian and Mr. C. was French and Mr. D. was Jewish. O.K. The switchboard at CBS lit up and stayed lit up for an hour with people complaining."

I jumped in armed with my one semester of sociology and yelled, triumphantly, "But you were wrong, for crying out loud. What kind of grouping is that?" Yahweh looked down (or up, I guess. I'm some inches taller; it just *seemed* down.)

"Come on, J. T. Get with it. Don't you think I know that? It was just a slip, for God's sake." (This from Yahweh.) Lennie was being patient, moving his palms down as though asking for a gradual pianissimo. "It was just a slip. But what a reaction! You think people don't have that stuff on their minds? Come on." And here he turned to Helen. "You know and you know you know." And she looked away.

Anyway, L. B. seemed to think the idea was a lot less provocative than when I had finished my pitch, and he sank back onto the sofa, assuring me that he had absolutely never in his life before been so tired. But he walked me to the door and said, as he massaged my back, solicitously, even though I wasn't in the least tired, that we would talk again. But we didn't, and in a month or so the Philharmonic had a new manager, and it wasn't J. T.

The new manager, the younger George Judd, took office, but in about two years died tragically young, and his associate, the brilliant Carlos Moseley, was named as his successor. And I got a call from Helen Coates asking me if I had any interest in being his assistant manager. Things at the Symphony being unduly horrible at the time, I said I would be interested, and she asked me to call Moseley, who was alerted. I did that, met with Carlos a few times (he told me that Bernstein had suggested that we spend a little time to see how we got on), and had him to dinner with my wife; we got along extremely well. Moseley is a superb musical administrator, and even more rare among full-time musical folk, an enormous intellect, with a prodigious knowledge of literature and art, and I will always treasure those days of our getting to know each other, preliminary to any possible professional association.

After some weeks, Carlos thought that I should meet the then chairman of the board of the Philharmonic, "the Boss," he called him. He was David M. Keiser. Moseley told me to call Keiser at his office to set up an appointment, and I was surprised to hear that he was president of the American-Cuban Sugar Company, and my surprise was occasioned by such a company existing a year or so after we had severed relations with Fidel and Cuban sugar. But I made a date and went up to see David M. Keiser at an old office building at Forty-second Street and Fifth Avenue, across the street from the Public Library. Here another surprise. The American-Cuban Sugar Company offices looked Dickensian. Item: all the men wore alpaca jackets; item: all the women were in competition for casting as Aunt Betsey Trotwood; item: there were high desks, I swear. Not many, but some high desks. And it was all dimly lit, dusty, and I had an eerie feeling that there was only a half-day off for Christmas.

Keiser was nondescript looking, middle-aged, graying, neither Dickensian nor non-Dickensian looking. He was neither friendly nor unfriendly; the interview was routine: where I went to school, my musical background, and so forth. I dragged in my army career for brownie points, only to get the no reaction that most of my exploits were getting. After I had gilded the lily a bit about my "success" in keeping the Symphony of the Air alive, he said, " 'Toobin,' what kind of a name is that?"

Well, the raconteur in me took over from the concerned citizen and instead of weighing the implications, if any, of that inquiry, I launched into one of my favorite monologues, repeated, I'm afraid, so often that if I ever lose my treasured wife, it could well be from a surfeit of monologues in general, but specifically from the oft-repeated "story of my name" in particular. "Good God," quoth my espoused saint, "not the one about your name again." Even my son, Jeffrey R. Toobin, fourteen, and reasonably respectful of his aged pater, has been known to admonish friends, of his and of mine, to be careful about the length of some of my anecdotes. And, ungrateful little whippersnapper, I once heard him tell a contemporary, while I was in mid-flight, "Oh boy, he's telling about his name again. My mom is going to have a fit."

"What kind of name is Toobin?"

Thus cued by Keiser, I launched into my tale.

My real name—that is, the name of my paternal grandfather, which is as far back as I can trace my lineage, was Tobachnick, which is Russian for tobacco-maker. My grandfather, who bore the sinister given name of Wolf (the Hebrew on which this was based is always translated in English as William, so why his name was Wolf has always been a fascinating mystery to me), came to the United States in the early part of the century and, as was the custom, changed the old-world patronymic—he became *Tobin*. Certainly, this latter was much more manageable than Tobachnick in day-to-day American life. But it had a flaw. Wolf's cronies informed him that *Tobin* was a common Irish-Catholic name, and hardly befitting a devout synagogue-hand, who even got up early to trot over for the morning worship. So, with a certain ingenuity, Wolf just slipped another o into *Tobin,* softening it, and certainly making it at least nondenominational. It is also, to the best of my knowledge, unique. I have looked at telephone directories in all parts of this country, its territories, and even in foreign lands, but I never found another *Toobin.*

All this I told David M. Keiser. He fell back into his usual torpor, as my scintillating foray into philology droned on, only once or twice, almost imperceptibly I thought, maybe wincing? Maybe frowning?

His first responsive words startled, and, alas, enlight-
ened me. "You mean your mother and father came from
Russia?"

I was startled mainly because I am certain I hadn't
mentioned my mother or father. Only Wolf, and the
metamorphosis that made Tobachnick into Toobin. So
I said, patiently, that my father had come here from the
Ukraine when he was six, and my mother was born in
North Philadelphia, not far from where I was to be born
somewhat later. And I don't know, I lost interest in the
interview, and shook hands with Keiser limply, and was
told there were many "excellent" applicants, and that
Mr. Moseley would be in touch with me.

I am only reporting this as it happened. It may or may
not be indicative of certain attitudes. Later, Carlos
Moseley told me that I was the last candidate eliminated
before his assistant manager was selected, and he never
said a word about anything David M. Keiser or anyone
else (including Leonard Bernstein, both of whose parents came from Russia) had said about me. It is just that
there were the little, but marked, reactions as I told
about the orgin of *Toobin,* and who knows, they may
have been induced by a spot of mustard ingested at
lunch. But as I walked through the antiquated offices of
the American-Cuban Sugar Company, passed the desk
of a lady who, though she was talking into a telephone,
had the gaunt, ravished, but aristocratic mien of Miss
Haversham, I couldn't help thinking that somehow my
story gave the impression that I was the scion of a Philadelphia branch of the then popular TV and radio
family, the Goldbergs, and that Mother *Toobin,* lately
come over from Kiev, would appear at the Philharmonic opening, undoubtedly in arch-support shoes, and

greet her friends across the entire width of Philharmonic Hall with a raucous, "Yoo-hoo, Mrs. Bloom, that
tall skinny one standing by the stage is my son, the
manager." After all, she couldn't be expected to be so
self-effacing as to say "assistant manager."

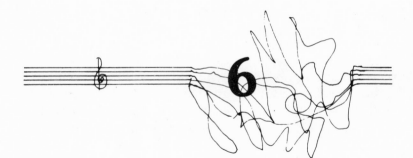

The best way to get money for an artistic venture is to have somebody give it to you. It is not necessary to cite the statistics on great American fortunes to make clear that there has been plenty of capital around in these states, and that historically some donors have sustained the so-called better things of life, among them music. Gustavus Myers in *The History of the Great American Fortunes* tells all too accurately the stories of the getting and the keeping of the fortunes, but there has always been the individual angel who has supported the arts lavishly. Probably the best known of these benefactors was Otto Kahn, the banker of the Kuhn, Loeb and Company empire, who among other things brought the Metropolitan Opera into its Golden Age in the early years of the century. He brought Gatti-Cassazza to New York from La Scala, and that impresario's first action was to make Toscanini principal conductor of the Met, no mean accomplishment. In fact Gatti, in his letter of acceptance to Kahn, made the engagement of Toscanini a condition of his own employment. Kahn was a man of sensitive and diversified tastes, who even helped the struggling and tortured Hart Crane, among others, though like many others he found it terribly difficult to do so.

The Lewisohns, Warburgs, Eastmans, Peabodys were among other well-known backers of musical enterprise. This account of the Symphony of the Air's fund-raising failures, however, is a glimpse at how some of today's rich, especially the younger breed, have risen to the challenge of assisting such struggling cultural entities as the Symphony of the Air. In a sense it almost has to be the younger that we are concerned with, because the substantial older fortunes which help the arts are pretty well tied up by the established cultural institutions. With the modern American tax structures, these old-line organizations and their individual wealthy donors have plenty of troubles of their own. But before taking up the individual backer, I would like to touch on some of the other fiscal instrumentalities by which the music business tries to stay alive.

The foundations have become a chief source of support for music these days, but that is a world of its own —a treacherous and at times whimsical one. I never penetrated it and so can't discuss it with any authority. And anyway I am discussing the ancient days of 1962 and earlier. One experience, however, was suggestive. As the Symphony was dying, I made a few attempts at getting short-range foundation help. One foundation functionary, an oily British type, who, as the DaVinci of free-loaders, was a New York institution (genius is the only term applicable to him for his gifts as a scrounger) attended all our concerts, all our parties, and when hard-pressed for diversion, even sat in on rehearsals. I went to him, at his eyrie on the umpteenth floor of some skyscraper owned by the public benefactor, to ask for $25,000. This sum was, as the commercial world has it, "to keep the doors open." He listened to me, having first made sure that the tickets would be at the box office for him. This latest set he was mooching was for a performance of the Brahms Requiem, which we were giving at Carnegie Hall. It seemed chillingly appropriate as one contemplated our prospects. The functionary looked very thoughtful. He brooded for about a minute while I tried superstitiously to influence his thought patterns by murmuring, "Give him the dough, give him the dough. . . ." I was about to make ingress into his hypothalamus when the *aficionado* of the Annie Oakley unpursed his lips and heaving a sigh said, "But my dear fellow, I haven't the slightest idea how I could get you that kind of money. You see we are geared for extensive programs, and there is no provision I know of for sums such as you mentioned."

He seemed to shudder just a little at the dimensions, or the lack of dimensions, of my request. A man used to lions probably reacts that way to mice and other wee beasties. Twenty-five thousand dollars seemed to give him the creeps. "Now if it were two or three million dollars," he continued, putting his hands out in a manner like a papal blessing, "we might have something to talk about."

I never knew if he was kidding or not; he was a humorless ass to start with, so I just thanked him, assured him the tickets would be at the box office, and was at the door. He stopped me. "Oh, dear boy, not too far to the left. It is a little dim for the basses, don't you know. On the aisle. That's a good chap." That was it. And I put him on the aisle. You never know.

Before tackling the rich and just asking them for their money, the artistic mendicant usually explores the wonderful world of the professional fund-raiser, he or she who lives by promoting food for the soul, playground facilities for the children of the ghetto, relief for any number of persecuted minorities in the always abundant locales where minorities are persecuted, and, here of late, is chiefly employed in getting monies to fight the polluted environment, the most virulent diseases of man, and that most profitable of modern scourges—smoking. And each of these crusades, with its armies of newspaper ads, magazine spreads, and TV commercials, are bonanzas for the money-raisers.

I was told by one of my army of advisers (one of the few things I was never short of) that one of the great names in public relations and fund-raising, Edward Bernays, was interested in the future of the Symphony of the Air, and I might do well to contact him.

Bernays was then living in the east Seventies, and he answered the phone most cordially. We set up an early meeting, and everyone I told about it was very sanguine, the gist of their opinions being that Bernays was a wonder man at conjuring up money.

Bernays was a husky, mustachioed man, then apparently in his sixties, tweedy, and very talkative. He spent the first few minutes regaling me with "me and Toscanini stories," none of them indicative of any great intimacy: things like seeing him in restaurants, hearing him conduct, and general gossip that I had heard innumerable times before. I listened patiently, for this, I was assured, was the financial Moses who would lead me out of my insolvent Egypt. After he had finished with the Maestro, he got on to Caruso, for whom he had done some promotional work in his salad days as a publicity man, and here, too, I was not fated to hear any startling material. Most of the stories concerned food: where

Caruso ate, how much he ate—a detailed culinary study of the great tenor. He was just giving me Caruso's favorite recipe for veal parmigiana when I may have betrayed, by an inadvertent stirring of some kind, that I was less than rapt. At any rate he then shifted to something crucial: Sigmund Freud.

Now anyone with even a rudimentary knowledge of the history of psychoanalysis knows that Frau Freud's maiden name was Martha Bernays. And, to be sure, the gentleman regaling me with statistics on the amount of pasta Caruso consumed in a week was the nephew of the founder of psychoanalysis. Sad to relate, one of the benighted without a rudimentary knowledge of the history of psychoanalysis was—and is—me. So that Bernays was a little less than delighted to apprehend that I wasn't following him when he began to talk about "my uncle." But once this fact had been established, and I had evinced a proper awe, Bernays went on to talk about Uncle Sigmund and to take me through the Freud room. This was an average-sized study, lined with fine bookcases built into the wall, and containing, I assume, almost the whole canon of Freud's work, in the original German and in translation. Bernays would take down a work, finger it, and make some comment about its material worth, while making clear that the value of the Freud room and its component parts was quite beyond calculation. And it was impressive. There is no question as to the extent of Freud's output, and to see this substantial library, stocked entirely with the works of one man, who in addition to his writing had a considerable practice as an analyst, many administrative duties, and time to indulge in innumerable differences with his disciples, was to be impressed.

But I had come there to talk about raising money, and after I had been with Bernays for almost two hours, I said, untruthfully, "This is really marvelous, Mr. Bernays, and I could spend a week in this room alone, but we have a rehearsal this afternoon and I hope we can talk about the Symphony." Making one last remark about the bindings on the French editions of Freud, and looking sorry for anyone who had to forego the pleasures he was bestowing (there was a sad little shake of his head that I remember), Bernays led me out of the sacred portals of the Freud room back to the workaday world of his office.

I reviewed the history of the orchestra, and the desperate state of its finances. He listened attentively, never interrupting to ask for any further information, and then proceeded to berate the city, the state, and the nation for letting this happen to us. He said he had not handled a fund-raising campaign for an artistic entity in quite a while, but he was very interested in helping us, and suggested a meeting again in a week to plan a campaign. He wanted to think more about it.

"But," he concluded hopefully, "we have to help you fellows. It is so unfair to think of you trying so hard to keep the Toscanini legend alive, and getting so little. Something's got to be done. Something has just *got* to be done." (He talked in slogans much of the time, and I can't remember most of them. But I know he repeated "the Toscanini legend" a great many times.)

A week later I was back, and while the extraneous matters took only about one hour this time (Galli-Curci, Paderewski, Babe Ruth, just a soupçon of Freud), I was disappointed to find that his cogitations were incomplete and that the next week we would *definitely* pro-

ceed to action. "We must preserve the Toscanini legend." I was beginning to get pretty damned sick of the
Toscanini legend à la Bernays by now, but I was in the
hands of the master and I was forced to look inspired by
his rhetorical flights. I did tell him on the way out that
things were really in a perilous state—our accountant
said that technically we had now been defunct for exactly a year, a gloomy anniversary if ever I heard of one.
The tax situation was reaching truly dangerous propor-
tions and so on and so on and so on! *Und so weiter,* Freud
would have said.

"We will prevail," Bernays assured me.

Things were finally resolved on my next visit. Bernays
looked cheery and bustled about the office as I settled
myself. There were no preliminaries. Right to the point.

"My boy, I've grown to like you a great deal; you are
a fighter. You are a fighter. [I was two fighters.] I'm a
fighter, and I like a fighter. And you are a fighter. [Three
fighters, four counting him, my distraught mind cal-
culated.] So I am going to help you and the orchestra. I
knew Toscanini and I admired him and he should be
remembered."

I idly wondered what he considered "knowing Toscanini," but even subconsciously I wasn't about to quib-
ble with the master. The hour had struck. He had said,
"I am going to help you."

"But you know" [and in retrospect I didn't like that
"but"], he went on, "this matter of fund-raising is a
science, and I am a believer, through my blood you
might say, in the scientific method. We must do this
right. This is a very important matter. Toscanini deserved nothing but the greatest effort when he was alive
and we must keep his legend alive. And I am resolved

to help you because I see quality in you. Here is what I'm going to do. I am going to make a complete and thorough survey of the potential for raising money for music in general and for your orchestra in particular. I will need to use most of my staff, and I will give it a great deal of personal attention. I like you, and I think you should be helped. So we will ask only five thousand dollars for the whole project."

Even as I recall that moment, I am forced to stop, as I did then, and try to believe what I heard. He was going to help us by charging *only* $5000 for a survey, which it was clear might show that he couldn't raise *any* money for us. For this I had sat through the Caruso, the Freud, the miscellany, and the resounding slogans. This was my time with the master. This was my baptism into the faith of the fund-raiser. Only $5000. That evening a call from our friend at Chase Manhattan informed us that our account was $211.27 overdrawn.

As a life-long devotee of baseball and football, I have had the admonition drummed into me, both as player and fan, to "capitalize on the breaks." Sometimes one can and sometimes one can't, but in our success-calibrated society it's the winners who do and the losers who don't. And there are no excuses. The Skouras story is an example of such a failure, and you can judge yourself whether or not I am making excuses.

The break was certainly there. One day in the winter of 1961, one of my advisers, a penurious lady-entrepreneur (at least she tried to be an entrepreneur) called me in great excitement to inform me that at a cocktail party the night before (she generally ate her dinner from the hors d'oeuvres cart of some crashable cocktail

party, of which there are generally quite a few every
night in Manhattan), she had been introduced to Mrs.
George Skouras. George was the brother of the fabled
Spyros, and while not a tycoon of that dimension, pretty
well fixed himself. After all, no Greek fortune is ever to
be ignored. Mrs. Skouras had a pet charity, the Boys
Towns of Italy, fashioned after the one we have in Nebraska, the brain child of Father Flanagan (or Spencer
Tracy, as he is better known). She talked to my operative
about fund-raising events, and that resourceful lady immediately announced that she was a representative of
the Symphony of the Air, and that it could be utilized
very effectively to raise money. (This was a very resourceful lady—imaginative, too.) She also bandied
about the name of Stokowski, who was indeed doing
most of the conducting with the orchestra then, and this
had an electrifying effect on Mrs. Skouras.

"You really think we could get Stokowski to conduct
for us?" she asked, incredulously. She was apparently
not too avid a music devotee because this—1958—was a
time when it was general knowledge that you could get
Stokowski to conduct for *anybody,* as long as you let
him conduct in New York. So my indomitable lieutenant, seeing a sizable commission in the undertaking,
made a luncheon date with Mrs. Skouras for the two of
us.

The luncheon was a sumptuous affair at the Colony,
where Mrs. Skouras was treated with a deference that
was both breath-taking and a little sickening. But I suppose that was the way it was when a Medici took some
artistic supplicant out to lunch in Renaissance Flor-
ence, so I quelled my egalitarian prejudices and decided
to relax and enjoy it. Mrs. Skouras still did not believe

that I could produce the great Stokowski and was all atremble even at the prospect. I casually (after having rehearsed the casualness all the way over in the cab) mentioned that I had spoken to the conductor that morning and that he had expressed great admiration for the Boys Towns of Italy and would conduct anywhere, any time, to help them. And I *had* spoken to Stokowski, who had said that he had never heard of the Italian Boys Towns, but that they sounded very worthy, and when was the concert and when could we get together to talk program. I made sure, for the record, that he understood that there was no fee attached, but Stokowski didn't care about that at this juncture in his career and concluded our conversation with a ringing nonsequitur. "I like the idea of these towns for poor boys; after all, I have two boys of my own." (The two boys, of course, were the sons of Stokowski and the former Miss Gloria Vanderbilt, the "poorest little-rich-girl in the world.") So I was fully armed as I sat at table with Mrs. Skouras and noted the eighth visit that hour from the maitre d' to make sure that everything was all right. It was fine.

I told Mrs. Skouras that I would talk program to Stokowski and get back to her with it and a budget. My Medici, apparently under the impression that she could charge practically anything for the privilege of hearing Stokowski, and helping the Boys Towns of Italy in the bargain, didn't blanch when I told her that the orchestral costs would be about ten thousand dollars, and marveled at her good fortune when I made the momentous announcement that Stokowski would donate his services.

The next day Mrs. Skouras called with the news that

Mario del Monaco, then the leading tenor of the Met (not an overwhelming distinction), had volunteered to appear on the program. I didn't know how this would sit with Stokowski, not exactly famous for sharing spotlights. I asked him about it, and he didn't seem to give it much thought, just saying that del Monaco shouldn't sing for more than ten minutes, which wasn't so bad. And he again pressed me to come over and talk program because he had, he said, "a wahndafooll idea." The "wahndafooll idea" was a little extreme even for my old hero from Philadelphia, who had, after all, really conducted one rehearsal with incense floating out over the orchestra, and another in a Japanese kimono. (The incense episode provoked an outburst from the magnificent first oboe, Marcel Tabuteau, an absolutely indispensable member of the Philadelphia orchestra in its greatest days. Tabuteau was a grumpy sort, famous as the cruelest teacher at the Curtis Institute, but his playing was peerless, and after all these years is, to my ears, still unmatched. He was a no-nonsense man and was not amused by some of Stoki's eccentricities. The incense was too much, making him sneeze for one thing, and he stood up and roared at Stoki in his heavily French-accented English, "You are crayzee—and you make us crayzee—," and with that he stormed off the stage. Not even Stoki could afford to lose Tabuteau, so the conductor went back stage and mollified the oboe player, who came back on stage grumbling, "He is still crayzee—.")

But Stokowski's idea for the Boys Town of Italy deserved a Nobel of the malapropos. Remember that the Boys Town was largely a project of the Catholic Church. The prime mover was the Right Reverend Monsignor

Patrick Carroll-Abbing. In fact the directorship of the Boys Town was half American high society and half Catholic clergy, not a bad start for a money-raising project. In this context came Stoki's idea.

"You know," said Stoki as he began our program meeting, "this sounds like a very important concert we are giving for the Italian Boys. And we must do something exciting and new." My heart was sinking rapidly, but it would have plummeted into Cousteau country if I had known what was coming. "I have received the newest symphony of Shostakovich, the Soviet composer. [He always threw in helpful little program notes like that.] It is about the Revolution in Russia in 1905. It is wahndafooll music and we should give it for the Italian boys. It is an American *première,* you know, and it will be very exciting."

Now Stoki knew very well that the Catholic Church was the principal body concerned with the "Italian boys." He had sat listlessly through a luncheon with the board of the Boys Towns, to which I had dragged him to prove that he was really available to them. The luncheon, except for Mrs. Skouras, my money-hungry aide-de-camp, two or three other ladies, and myself, was peopled entirely by priests. Why, I thought, recalling the dismal luncheon at which hardly anybody said anything, and only the reiterated boot-licking of the maitre d' broke the gloomy silence, why didn't he say something then about the Shostakovich and the Revolution of 1905? But no, this delight was saved for me—all for me—and I had to pass on to the ladies and the priests the glorious news that Stoki was going to regale them with a one-hour-and-fifteen-minute symphony, whose movements are titled:

I   *The Palace Square.*

II   *January 9*——The workers of St. Petersburg
march through the streets toward the Palace
Square.

III   *Eternal Memory*——The funeral procession,
mourning the victims that fell on "Bloody Sunday"—January 9.

IV   *Alarm*——The alarm is sounded throughout work-
ing-class Russia. The people come to understand their aim clearly, and they will be united
in the spirit of uprising which will bring them
to ultimate victory in the Socialist Revolution
of 1917.

Now I must hasten to give it as my opinion that Stokowski was not being malicious or political in his desire
to perform the Shostakovich. In my rare political discussions with him, he had professed ignorance of political matters, and he never did anything to make me
doubt his self-judgment. In Philadelphia, a long time
before—in the early thirties—he had caused some political stirrings on the American Legion Right by such
actions as having the Youth Concert audience sing the
Internationale as one of a long series of national an-
thems. He had stirred the same type of reactionary ire
by joining a welcoming committee when the French
writer Henri Barbusse came to Philadelphia, but practically all of the city's cultural luminaries were on the
committee, and he wasn't going against any popular
tide by helping to honor an internationally important
literary figure. His political sophistication was summed
up for me in 1960 when I asked him what he thought of
the presidential race between Kennedy and Nixon. He
had an opinion this time. "I like this Kennedy, he seems

like a good man, and he is young. But I don't like the Jesuits. I never trust the Jesuits. If Kennedy says that he will leave the Catholic Church, I will vote for him."

I thought of the moment when this startling proposition would be brought before candidate Kennedy, and the masses in the various Catholic strongholds, as the papers call them. That was a clue to Stokowski's political sophistication, and I believe him about being apolitical. Concerning his anti-Jesuitical sentiments, I knew there had always been some mystery about Stokowski's religious origins—along with the mystery of his origins in general. He was once talking to me about the difficulty of answering children when, as they inevitably do, they ask about God. He said, "I don't know what to say, do you? I'm a Catholic, but a bad one, and this is too difficult for me to explain even to myself." And that is all I ever heard from him on that score. But I feel certain that the main reason, indeed the only reason, that he had for programing the Shostakovich was the public interest it would engender. After all, Stokowski had been out of the limelight for quite a while by 1958, and this major *première* was a good opportunity to attract attention. The propriety of the action, however, is harder for me to evaluate. The concert was being held for what was basically a Catholic charity, and the intent was to raise as much money as possible for that cause. I must say that never, in any of the alarums that followed, did anyone of the Boys Town group, lay or clerical, object to the Shostakovich per se or mention the programmatic content of the work. Their chief objection, explicitly, at least, was that new music never draws, and that the great length of the work precluded any major popular elements in the concert. Del Monaco was going to sing, but only for ten minutes; and with a ninety-minute symphony only about a half hour of other music was possible. It was a tough nut.

First simple remedies were tried. The committee just asked that I simply tell Stokowski that it would be very hard to fill the house at an escalated scale of prices with a new work. One of the ladies, an alumna of Stoki's Philadelphia period, said, "Tell him he played the Brahms Second better than any conductor that ever lived, and if he does that at the concert, we have a sell-out." There were other similar feeble suggestions as to how to get the great man to change his mind, and it was left to me to bring about the miracle.

I went to see Stokowski and tried the Brahms gambit. He listened, and showed no emotion at all through my whole narrative, even when I was quite candid in saying that I thought it would be very hard to get a big audience for a new symphony, although, of course, if anyone in the world could, it was Stokowski. I said this knowing very well that Stokowski was not drawing in New York no matter what the program, but this was a minor duplicity, I felt. Finally, I finished, sensing that I had done poorly. Stokowski answered.

"You are absolutely right. It is terrible but it is true. There are ten million people in New York, and yet we can't get an audience for a new important work. And you are right about the Brahms. I love that music. What genius went into it. I love to conduct that work. So you are right, and your people are right. It would make a beautiful concert. So you get another conductor, there are hundreds of them, and you can have the Brahms."

Pure Stokowski. The completely unexpected twist. Not to me though. I had been a Stokowski watcher too long to expect anything but the unexpected. I wasn't puffed up by his series of "you're rights." I know this much about Stokowski at least. If he wants something, he is going to get it. And if you stand in the way, either you or he will go away. "Get another conductor." How many times had I heard those words? So I went back to my priests and my ladies, and we prepared for the Herculean (Sisyphean, I suspected) task before us. And it all turned out just as badly as I feared it would.

There is no point in going into all the things that went as wrong as expected. Some of the developments however were extreme by any standard. For one thing, two weeks or so before the concert New York had one of its periodic newspaper strikes, and it lasted until after the event. This accomplished the following: 1) no newspaper publicity or advertising, except for direct-contact promotion and a little radio and TV, plus a few sad little ads in the *Christian Science Monitor* and the *Wall Street Journal,* which continued to appear during the strike, so that as far as the general public was concerned, the concert was a well-kept secret; 2) all of Stokowski's plans for vast publicizing and discussion of the Shostakovich *première* went aglimmering. There was a lengthy review in *The New Yorker* by Winthrop Sargeant calling his latest symphony final proof, to Sargeant, that the wells of Shostakovich's creativity had completely dried, and that he couldn't imagine why Stokowski had gone to the trouble of performing it. Personally I thought it fairly effective movie music, and my opinion was borne out when it was used for exactly that purpose in a new version of Eisenstein's *Ten Days That Shook the World,* a film which I couldn't judge objectively because the sound track kept jarring me back inexorably to the days that shook my world around the time of the Italian boys concert.

The concert drew badly, del Monaco was in poor voice, and Stokowski treated del Monaco rudely, shooing him off stage right after his tenth allotted minute and not even letting him get the semblance of an ovation (little remnants of his Metropolitan claque had somehow found their way into Carnegie). Everyone on the administrative end of things—ladies, priests, and I —felt perfectly miserable. Of course my principal chagrin was occasioned by the failure of Mrs. Skouras in her debut in the music business. I had plans to talk to her about future events, benefits for that most worthy of all charities, the Symphony of the Air, and even a hare-brained scheme to have her introduce me to her renowned brother-in-law, the regal Spyros, and getting S. S. (as he's known in the movie biz) to use the orchestra for the musical scores in Twentieth-Century-Fox pictures. The fact that S. S. didn't show up at the concert made the latter scheme even harder to accomplish than it would normally have been. No, I had had a great break, and I hadn't capitalized on it. Mrs. Skouras was dropped out of heaven, right at my feet, and I had proceeded to assist her in a fund-raising project that *lost* money. One of the reasons for this calamitous result was the fact the orchestra required for the Shostakovich was huge—110 players (8 percussionists for one thing; revolutions are generally noisy) and the costs for the orchestra alone exceeded fifteen thousand dollars. This was about twice the cost of an average concert.

I never saw much of Mrs. Skouras any more, although my contact still pursued her (she got another lunch or two at the Colony), undeterred by the fact that her commission for the Boys Town concert was the privilege of sitting in one of the many empty seats, and all she could eat at the party afterward. A gloomy affair that was.

My most vivid memory of the concert, though, is of the many, many clergy, sitting rather stiffly, and seemingly absorbed, as Stokowski on-stage was whipping the orchestra through the deafening finale, with its drums and cymbals simulating all kinds of ordnance. And in each pair of clerical hands a program was held, containing in its pages the information that this music represented "the spirit of uprising which will bring ... ultimate victory in the Revolution of 1917."

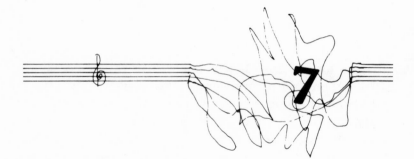

Even as Mrs. Skouras thought the great name and fame of Leopold Stokowski would mean heavy revenues for the Boys Towns of Italy, so did I turn to one of the mighty for assistance. In 1958 Mme. Maria Callas was staying in New York for a few days negotiating with Rudolph Bing about some appearances with the Metropolitan. She was then, as now, one of the fabled of the musical world, with the difference that then she was active and accepted a few carefully selected engagements, while now she very rarely makes a public appearance. One of the most brilliant artistic strategists in history, Mme. Callas was able to project an average voice, great dramatic ability, and superb musicianship into a great career. Interestingly, by the time she achieved fame, her voice was past its prime, but she husbanded it carefully and by judiciously spacing her appearances—she was the supreme example of the benefits of underexposure—made all of her engagements major events. And she was amazing; taking such familiar parts as Lucia, Norma, and Violetta, she made thrilling experiences of them. All this without a voice that could produce the incredible sounds that made legends of Tetrazzini, Galli-Curci, and Joan Sutherland. Alas, an occasional Callas shriek was incredible for quite different reasons. But the overall performance was generally of such emotional intensity and musical purity that she may have been the greatest singing actress of her time.

But that wasn't the reason I sought an audience with her. I quite simply wanted to exploit her enormous powers at the box office. I felt, in my deep financial need, that I would be quite irresistible when I threw myself on her tender mercies and implored her to save the Symphony by singing some arias at a special concert. Stokowski, ever ready to make the New York scene, expressed an eagerness to conduct such a concert, even though my recent Skouras debacle made me hesitate. I had visions of Stoki programing the Bach B Minor Mass, and letting Callas appear at about eleven thirty or midnight to sing one aria and "Home Sweet Home." Or maybe one of Chairman Mao's composers had a new little opus, running two hours or so, that Stoki thought would stir up some newspaper talk. No, this was to be Callas's night (and by extension mine), because if there was one artist who you could be certain would fill any hall, anywhere in the Western world, and at any price, it was *La Divina,* as she is known to the gallery gods. (The term isn't made inappropriate by the tale, possibly apocryphal, that she made it up herself.)

Mme. Callas was staying at one of the poshest hotels in the world, and I got to her by doing some extensive research in the telephone directory. I called the hotel, asked for her, and she was on the line in a second. I bandied about the name of Toscanini with whom, as far as I knew, she had never worked, but the old magic worked, and she said she would be glad to see me without even asking what I wanted. The date was for the rather improbable time of Saturday evening at 8:00 p.m., but it made for a certain piquancy when I told my date of the evening (these were the waning days of my bachelorhood) that I would be late, because, "I have to see Callas."

I went to her suite, a small and modest one, and was admitted by her husband, since departed—as a husband, that is—Signor Meneghini. He was a tycoon of some sort—pasta, I think—a gray, tall, kindly man, who asked me immediately if I spoke Italian. I answered that I did a little, a very little, and he laughed and said that a very little Italian was *bastante*. I was immediately ushered into the Great Presence; the Great Presence, sitting on a little divan, was clutching the tiniest poodle I've ever seen. She was dressed very simply, in a skirt, sweater, ballet slippers, with just globs of eye makeup I didn't need even a little Italian with Mme. Callas, for Brooklyn born and bred, this great lady of the opera spoke wholesome, unaffected New Yorkese. She put out her hand, still clutching the almost invisible poodle. I sat in a large armchair at her right hand, and I had no sooner settled myself when the poodle popped right out of her grasp and into my lap. It snuggled there, while I squirmed. But the happening seemed to electrify Callas.

"Oh, you're a good person. You're a good person," she cried in an ascending scale. And she grabbed my hands. I was now squirming with a poodle snuggled in my lap, and holding hands with Maria Callas—easily the most unlikely moment in a life (mine, that is) not unaccustomed to the bizarre. "She never goes to any one. Never. And you walk in, and right away she goes to you. You must be a very good person."

My theory was that living at that time on the East Side

of Manhattan, dog-metropolis of the universe, I just always smelled of dog, even though I myself didn't own one. But I was quite content to let Mme. Callas believe she had just admitted a votive of St. Francis of Assisi into her temporary home. It certainly got things off beautifully. My style was to try to find some personal tie with the potential donor, for my whole existence at this time seemed to be taken up with supplication, and I was always asking for something—money, generally, but as with Callas, it could be the use of supreme musical gifts for what I considered a noble cause. With Callas I mentioned Cantelli, whom I knew she had sung with fairly recently, just before his death.

"Oh that poor boy," she commiserated, "he had no luck at all. None at all. [She was a great repeater.] And you know about it, I suppose. You must know about it." She looked mysterious and ominous. The tremendous eye shadow and her very sharp features made her look like some Egyptian oracle foretelling imminent and hideous doom. I was almost afraid to pursue the matter further. I had been a friend of Cantelli's, I had admired him as man and artist, and I didn't want to hear anything ugly about him now, with his death still troubling and depressing me. But she pressed on. "You look like you don't know. You really look like you don't know." I wanted to escape this terrible revelation. My mind raced, conjuring up horrible possibilities—personal, artistic. "I think you should know. You were his friend." She would not be denied. I braced myself. "He didn't have any insurance. Not a penny. Not one penny."

As her bombshell exploded, she sat back, her arms folded (no mean trick considering she was again holding the puppy in some remarkably dextrous way). She

waited for my incredulity to manifest itself—I guess she
expected some sign of amazement at Cantelli's incom-
prehensible conduct. I, relieved beyond words, just sat
there. In addition, and I think this hurt in the eventual
negotiations, I even grinned. I couldn't help it. After that
build-up. After my anxieties for the good name of my
beloved friend. She continued, "We Italians [I knew she
was Greek, but I guess she considered herself a spiritual
Italian] don't believe much in thinking about the future,
and we don't believe much in insurance. But that boy
was a new father, and he was too young to have made
much. How could he have done such a thing." And she
shook her head wearily.

I thought as I looked at her of Matthew Arnold's lines:

> Sophocles long ago
> Heard it on the Aegean, and it brought
> Into his mind the turbid ebb and flow
> Of human misery. . . .

This great singer, whose manner was all intensity and
drama, even though she looked for all the world like
thousands of other Latin girls I had seen on the streets
of American cities, seemed to be bemoaning the ulti-
mately tragic fate of the race as she thought of how
Cantelli had ignored insurance. Her last words on the
subject. "Not one penny, can you imagine?"

Now to business. "And what do you want from me?"

Long exposition of her wonders as artist and woman.
Long wordy analogy between her greatness and Toscanini's. Simply truthful declaration that she was probably the world's greatest musical attraction. (Slightest
tremor of the eyebrow in the sea of mascara at the use
of the adverb "probably.") Finally, the direct plea for a

great benefit concert, historical in content and effect, at
which New York would hear *La Divina* in an evening
of her greatest arias, showing her unequaled versatility
—Turandot, Mimi, Isolde, maybe even Gershwin's Bess
—with a great orchestra and a great conductor. I didn't
mention *him*. She was obviously going to be enough to
handle without having to cope with Stoki, too. I would
come up with *some* great conductor, even if his greatness was transient. She listened. She didn't react, except
fleetingly to the "probably."

"Thank you. I try. But you know, I'm very, very expensive."

"And you deserve even more than you get. But this is
the one chance for the orchestra to make enough money
to live on for a while. Only you can do it. And I'm sure
you know that." Why in the hell did I say "probably"
before. If I had been a judge, I would have struck it from
the record.

"Miss Tebaldi sang with you last season, didn't she?
And I know what you paid her. And I always get much
more than Miss Tebaldi."

There it was. This insane business of music. *She* knew
how much Tebaldi—excuse me, *Miss* Tebaldi—got last
season. (Her reiterated use of "Miss" for the superb
Renata was always uttered in a condescending manner
that made it sound like the "sirrah" the Elizabethans
reserved for fools and knaves.) I couldn't resist.

"Tell me, Madame Callas, how much do you think we
paid Tebaldi?" (I refused to play her game. No Miss for
me. I adored Tebaldi. I had a little pride left.)

She told me. Right to the penny. It was by no means
Tebaldi's regular fee. It had been arranged through
Bernstein, who conducted a concert with Tebaldi and

Bjoerling doing Puccini excerpts. It was a big favor to Bernstein and the orchestra, and no one in the world was to know about it. I didn't tell my girl friend, my mother, my trusted assistant, Stewart Warkow. Such secrecy went out with the Manhattan Project. But Callas, who had been in America maybe for two weeks between that year-old concert and this meeting, knew what Tebaldi got—to the penny. And it was an uneven amount. Astounding. I tried to talk around the Tebaldi matter: I first tried to imply, and then I baldly stated that Callas was in a class by herself and that comparisons with any other artists were impossible.

"Oh, Miss Tebaldi is a good singer," she said, looking up at me with a little twinkle, I think. She really used lots of mascara.

But I wasn't getting into that. I just kept hammering away at Callas's uniqueness and her indispensability as a lifesaving agent for the orchestra. She suddenly changed the subject.

"So what do you think of Bernstein, your Lenny?" (He wasn't my Lenny, but she was certainly from Brooklyn. Every nuance.)

Now that is one of the most often asked questions in the music business. There are usually one of two answers: this held a decade ago as I spoke to Callas; this still holds today.

1 / For Bernstein adulators: "He's a genius."

2 / For those who don't think he represents the Second Coming, and wonder what exactly he's a genius at: "He's very talented."

I said to Callas, "He's very talented."

"Yes but he is very peculiar. I just sang Cherubini's

Medea with him at La Scala. And at first everybody was thrilled, just thrilled. Especially the orchestra, and you know what crabs they are. [I knew.] They said he knew every note, and his Italian was good, and it was fine. But at the second rehearsal he came back after the break, and he had both hands full of candy, little pieces of candy. And he began throwing them out into the orchestra. And the musicians don't know what to do. Try to catch them, dive after them, what should they have done? He would throw a piece of candy, and he would throw a kiss, and another piece of candy. He wanted to show them how pleased he was, or something. All these old La Scala men sitting there and the maestro [and she covered her face with her hand as she giggled, the dog bouncing into my lap again] throwing kisses and candy. He's something, your Lenny." (I think she meant the country-at-large's Lenny.)

Signor Meneghini, who had sat with us in the early moments of our talk, but beat a quiet, yet hasty retreat when his wife evinced her ecstasy over the poodle's recognition of my virtue, now tiptoed in and whispered something to her in Italian. She seemed impatient and waved him away. This was flattering because she told me that he was always worrying about time, and Kurt Adler of the San Francisco Opera was due in a few minutes. But she was enjoying our conversation and, she added acerbically, "I'll be damned if I'll hurry for any manager. [I didn't know where that left me, but I was still flattered. That poodle sure knew quality.] These opera managers. All sugar and spice when they want you to sing for them, but afterwards all they want to talk about is saving money on rehearsals. Your Mr. Bing, too. [Now he was *my* Mr. Bing and I had never even met the man.] Him and his lousy, drafty stage. I get a cold every time I step onto it." And she shuddered, remembering.

"So what do we do. What do we do. I'd like to help you, but I have so little time, and I get so many requests to do things to help people. And don't worry. Everybody in our business is going broke." I wasn't worried about people going broke, I *was* broke. My accountant had assured me of it. It was like a cold-hearted doctor informing some next-of-kin that while the body still functioned, the patient was "clinically" dead. I was engaged in a task of resurrection. "Going broke" was in the past. I was trying to conjure up an orchestral Lazarus. I told her some of this, but without the theological references because I was certain she was more at home in the world of the accountant.

Then the usual ominous denouement: "Let me think about it. I'll call you in a few days." I figured I had failed again. My Lazarus was just going to lie there. As a miracle worker I was an all-American bust. Signor Meneghini saw me out. I said a few words in Italian. He smiled benignly and said that I was pretty good and that I should practice. As I left I caught one last glimpse of *La Divina* in the sitting room. She was talking earnestly to the poodle, which she held out in front of her at arms' length. Smallest poodle I've ever seen.

I had about forgotten Callas as a source of help, when, four or five days later, I returned from lunch to some astounding news. Our telephone operator–bookkeeper–publicity assistant–typist–file clerk–maintenance manager—all a pretty, harried little girl named Janice Kurtis, who had come in to help out one afternoon during a flu epidemic and stayed for six years—said, "Sit down. You'll have to when I tell you this one. An hour ago the phone rang, and a lady on the other end said, 'Hello. This is C-a-l-l-a-s. Is Mr. Toobin there.' No kidding. She spelled the name out. Every letter. I made sure it was no joke. [I still don't know how she did that.] She wants you to call her." Ever resourceful, Janice was dialing even as she finished her message. I grabbed the phone. Signor Meneghini said in his soft voice that his wife would be right with me.

"I've been thinking about our talk," she said. "I have to go to Chicago tomorrow. The case with that son of a bitch is coming up. Write me a letter. Tell me what you propose, and we'll meet again." For the record, the case with "that son of a bitch" was a widely publicized suit by a smalltime agent who had somehow gotten Callas in her youth—her childhood, practically—to sign a contract guaranteeing him a share of her earnings in perpetuity. He of course never did a thing for her, "not even an 'Oh Promise Me' at a wedding," Callas recalled, but after she became famous, he and his felonious contract showed up, demanding millions. Callas won the case in a walk, but she did have to go to Chicago; she did not return to New York again for months, and when she did she went back onto Mr. Bing's "lousy, drafty stage" for a few Normas, and all my efforts to reach her were in vain. Signor Meneghini was gone by then, and every time we called, there was no answer. Messages went unanswered, too, and that was that for another of my grandiose attempts at a detour on the road to oblivion.

Once when we were working with Sir Thomas Beecham, he mentioned *Les Troyens* of Berlioz and said how he would love to put it on some day. Then the baronet exploded, his normal manner of expression. "And you know who I'd put in as Dido? Old lady Callas.

There's a girl. Never know if she's going to show up or not for the damned performance. [Strange virtue I thought, but the baronet had exotic tastes.] But we'll never get her any more. For I do believe, she is now devoting herself entirely to the ensnarement of Mr. Onassis." *La Divina* was apparently no more successful in that endeavor than I was in mine. But who knows, perhaps the final returns on her quest are not yet in. Those on mine are.

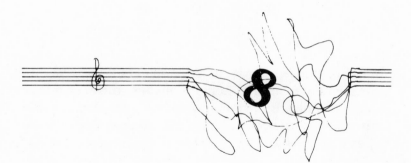

I must now come, with some reluctance, to the
rich, the benefactors who can by the simple act of writing a check make it possible for the artist to do the
things he spends his life preparing for: keeping the
great traditions of the past alive and creating the works
that will reflect the past and anticipate the future. In
music, a symphony orchestra is integral to these pro-
cesses. The Medicis served the arts, as did the Borgias
and the Esterhazys—and none of them were particularly admirable folk. But they gave great artists oppor-
tunities to work. The Symphony's experiences were
with equally unadmirable folk, most of the time.

For years potential orchestra saviors would come and
go. Important names would be dropped to me by well-
wishers and busybodies with the assurance that if they
were cultivated, these affluent ones, they would lighten,
if not remove, the burden of poverty which encumbered
the orchestra. We would provide them with the best
seats for our concerts; they would be invited to the post-
concert parties which are *de rigueur* for any musical
event of any stature in New York; they would be imbued
with a full appreciation of their importance to the cultural community. The names received were impressive
enough; they were found on the hoods of automobiles,

on the facades of textile plants and cereal factories, on household utensils and home remedies, and even on the doors of banks. But, somehow, after refreshments, the chitchat, and the obtaining of the autographs of name soloists and conductors for star-struck young relatives, there was nothing. The important contacts would shun personal meetings; letters pleading for funds to combat some dire emergency were answered with five- and ten-dollar contributions, when they weren't ignored altogether. Beyond the mounting debts and the ferocious creditors, most ominous of all our dilemmas was the inability to hold the best players without guaranteeing them adequate employment. The orchestra was quite simply beginning to disintegrate.

But, lo, in the winter of 1960 a Messiah was brought into our midst. This Messiah was a North Carolinian in his late twenties, pale, blondish, of medium height, thin, with a submerged quality of intensity. I had known these types in the arts before—at least with this manner of volcanic heat under a refined and subdued exterior. Some were very difficult and very creative. Some were mad and dangerous. I decided to put analyses and intuitions behind me because for each time I had been right in my instant attempts at judging externals, I had been wrong another. Generally, I held with the cliché of books and their covers.

The Messiah came to us by way of the lady who brought us Mrs. Skouras. While that record was hardly an augury of success, there had been so many extenuating circumstances in the Skouras debacle that no blame could adhere to the "lady of the contacts," as I shall call her. She was a woman who had probably been beautiful a decade or so before. Now a divorcée with three children, she was belatedly trying to make her fortune by making her habitat the gathering places of the rich, while attempting to drum up projects that would divert them and feed her and her brood. She was appealing enough as she made her rounds looking for the main chance, but too devious and desperate to trust for any length of time. But she was a cheery optimist, a Mediterranean lady-Micawber, certain that something would turn up in her wealth-engirdled milieu which would end her penury and save the orchestra at the same time. For some reason, she was convinced that this poverty-stricken, probably doomed Symphony was her vehicle for a ride to glory. And like Barkis, we were all too willin'. Some of the great alliances in history were born of interlocking self-interests. And the lady came leading a Messiah.

A tea was arranged by "the lady of the contacts," in her shabby-genteel West Side apartment for the Messiah and me. My constant companion Stewart Warkow came as my second and there was one other participant. This was a handsome, dark, almost Arabic-looking boy. He seemed at most twenty-one, tall, very well built, introduced as a friend of the Messiah who "was studying singing." Hereafter it must be understood that he and the Messiah were always together, indeed were living together in an apartment in the East Sixties. It must further be understood that in all the times I saw him, and it was very many times, I never heard the would-be singer say anything of substance—never. He would say hellos and good-byes; he would murmur (he would always murmur) in a pleasant voice, "Yes, thank you," or "No, thank you," when food was passed. He would say, "Cream, no sugar," or "Mmm," when someone remarked on the excellence of the hors d'oeuvres. He would say "very," and it came out musically, when someone said it was hot out or cold. And that was it. But he was always there.

We will call the Messiah Bill Montgomery. His real name was the same kind of nondescript American one, derived from the English, which we hear all day long, attached to a baseball star, a shoeshine boy, or a textile millionaire's son. Bill was the latter.

He seemed to do nothing—besides saving the Symphony, that is. He carried with him to the tea at the "lady's" a short story he had written, and which had appeared in the *Atlantic* five years before. He said he had written it while he was living in Paris. It was very short, a page or so; what used to be called a "short, short." I don't remember what it was about, the plot that is. There was a dog in it; it took place in the North Carolina hill country, and the protagonist was a boy about ten. But I don't remember what happened to any of them.

Bill said he loved music, he *adored* it, he could not live without it. He said, "I must have music with me at all times." I remember thinking of the gentlewoman's comment about Lady Macbeth in the sleepwalking scene: "she has light by her continually; 'tis her command." There was something eerie about the way Bill was talking about music, as though he would have it by command. There was that strange compulsive quality. But again I shook off parlor psychoanalysis to contemplate instead my incipient good fortune. Bill had heard the Symphony of the Air, he told me, and found it excellent. (I wondered if the "lady" had taken him to the Skouras concert to share the Revolution of 1905 with the clergy.)

He spoke with a very slight southern accent, which I shall not bother to phoneticize, since it didn't flavor his speech. He was actually not at all communicative, and I couldn't ascertain if he knew anything about music, the art or the business. But he *adored* it. Early in the talk he asked if Stokowski was our regular conductor. (He called him Sta-cow-ski, and did so to the very end, even though I told him that the conductor took offense at that pronunciation.) I told Bill that Stokowski wasn't officially connected with the orchestra but that he did the majority of our engagements and most of our recordings.

Then he matter-of-factly told me his plan. Bill wanted the orchestra, first, to go on a tour of Europe the coming spring. The orchestra would visit London, Paris, Amsterdam, some other world capitals, and a few comparatively out-of-the-way places like Rouen, Bari, and Strasbourg. Nothing, he made clear, in Eastern Europe or the Soviet Union. The climax of the tour—of five weeks' duration—was to be a pair of concerts at the Vatican. He was arranging for this, he said, because he knew that Pope John XXIII was a great music-lover and would gladly host the concerts. Stokowski was to be the conductor. We would then, after the tour that is, organize the first regular season of the Symphony for the following fall: about twenty weeks, Stokowski as the principal conductor, "and some others." He was well prepared, it seemed, and from some promptings she gave him, I sensed that the "lady" had been talking to him. In fact one of his first administrative decisions—he was to be president of the new organization—was that the "lady" was to become public-relations director. He was working on choosing a board of directors, with many of the same people to be sponsors of the European tour. I would continue to function as manager of the orchestra. All this was done in a mild and unautocratic style. He made clear that he would run the show, quite clear, but he would be the most benevolent of rulers. And he would underwrite all the costs for tour and season.

The plan to make the Symphony of the Air the second major orchestra in New York was of paramount interest to us. To our delight, Bill made much of this concept in our earliest conversations. The question of *another* major orchestra in New York had been under fervent discussion by us long before Bill Montgomery came up from North Carolina. Our publicity stressed the point that most of the great cities of the world had at least two, and in many cases more than two, orchestras: London, Paris (creaky though some of them were), Moscow, Vienna, Berlin, and so on.

(In 1956, Giovanni Gronchi, then president of Italy, came to the United States. In New York he was tendered a reception to which Cantelli took me. The conductor introduced me to President Gronchi, who was knowledgeable in musical matters. He was told that I was managing what was left of Toscanini's orchestra and that our financial status was precarious. When I gave it as my candid opinion that the ultimate chances of our survival were slim, he seemed actually to disbelieve me, or at least to misunderstand. He put it this way: "My little Rome has two regular orchestras, I think, maybe more. They are not great orchestras as you have here. They are good but not great. And if in Rome we can do it, how can it be that in New York there is no room for Maestro Toscanini's orchestra? I find it hard to understand." So did I.)

Bill Montgomery, in addition to his enthusiasm for the Symphony of the Air, seemed very resentful toward the "other" orchestra in town, the Philharmonic. I suspected why, and a little probing substantiated my suspicions. He had obviously tried to crack the stratified social structure that is the Philharmonic family, a vintage group which, with its ancestors, has helped pay the bills since the orchestra was organized in 1842. To be a Philharmonic bigwig is to be a very solid part of the New York cultural establishment. Montgomery, eager to make his mark socially in the big city, had apparently found the going rough in Philharmonic country, and indeed it *is* treacherous terrain. He constantly made such peevish remarks as, "Those old fuddy-duddies over there at the Philharmonic that wouldn't know a good idea if it reared up and bit them"; or, "The Philharmonic is a mausoleum, not an orchestra." It was obvious that he had failed in his endeavors to enter the realm of the "fuddy-duddies." But I had no false pride on that score; I would take all the millionaire discards the Philharmonic sent my way.

Bill listed the names he had accumulated to act as sponsors for the tour and assured me that they would all agree to serve on the board of the orchestra for next year's season. Honorary chairman was Senator Sam Ervin of North Carolina. I had never heard that gentleman's name being linked with the arts before, but a little local pride was not amiss, and Bill told us that he had known the senator all his life. "Senator Sam," he called him. Other members of the sponsor's group included Cardinal Spellman, Mrs. Claire Booth Luce, the Prince of Monaco and the Princess, the former Grace Kelly, another prince and princess with Russian names, whom I had never heard of, and, of all people, Jackie Gleason. I never inquired into how this variegated list was put together, but Bill had letters from every one of them corroborating the fact of their acceptance of a post in Bill's organization. As time went on, other celebrities joined the sponsor's list, the kind that join anything that seems sure to make *The New York Times,* so long as the cause in question is noncontroversial enough.

I told Stokowski about the tour, about Bill, and about the latter's desire that Stokowski be the conductor. He never said he agreed, or discussed terms; he just went right to work. "We must make programs that are good for the countries we will visit. We should have two or three programs. Time will be too short for us to have any soloists. We must get the best players in the world for this tour. I knew the pope in Venice many years ago; he loves music." And so on. Stokowski was ready.

Bill was businesslike in the early days of the project, even doing such menial chores as checking the accuracy of mailing lists and going over budgets with me. He always maintained a certain hauteur about these material matters, as though he was conscious they were demeaning, but he did them as though they were part of a work ethic that was spiritually rewarding. St. Joan washing dishes, that sort of thing.

I took Bill to meet Stokowski. Bill said very little, but he was by no means awed by the famous conductor. He seemed a trifle bored and impatient until the fifteen-minute conference was over. Bill would lounge in his chair at most meetings, and this one was no exception. I can only describe his manner as languorous. He seemed not only confident, but *au-dessus de la bataille.*

Bill used to play on us all like some master organist:

everyone was part of a gigantic keyboard and as Bill struck us, we became part of a celestial harmony that he held in his superior mind. Occasionally, when I would try to bring him down from his ethereal organ-loft with some mundane matter like the need to post some monies with the Musicians' Union as a bond on our intentions, he would grow a little irritable, but his equanimity would soon return, and he would go back to treating the earthlings around him with remote kindness. And the nearly mute disciple would always be with the master, a vague presence, to whom, however, the master would seem to address most of his remarks. It would make a weird scene: Bill would be talking ostensibly to me about orchestra players, but he would be looking right at the silent one; and when I would answer, awkwardly under the circumstances, he would again respond to the silent one. This would happen with everyone and was particularly notable at this first Stokowski meeting. The silent one was of course there.

Whereas Bill was taciturn at this session, Stoki was very talkative. He was uttering thunderous platitudes about how music would insure world peace if only more orchestras toured. Bill would nod at the silent one and murmur assent: "Yes, I guess it would."

I was being made acutely uncomfortable by Bill's refusal to face anyone but his all-but-catatonic roommate and felt like enlivening the proceedings. To block out Stoki's less-than-immortal utterances and the bizarre manners of Bill, my mind wandered, and I thought I should ask Stoki, apropos the peace-inducing nature of music, about that well-known German music-lover A. Hitler. Herr Hitler's passion for music ranged from the Wagnerian music dramas, which were moth-

er's milk to him, to the *Merry Widow,* which he saw over
a hundred times. *There* was a peace-promoter for you.
But I restrained the impulse, chiefly because I knew I
was just taking out my peevishness at the weird Stoki-
Bill meeting on everything and everyone, even music.
So I mused as Stoki brought the conference to a close
with a lofty peroration to the effect that people all over
the world were alike, and that if they listened to music,
they would learn to love one another. That is why this
tour was a good thing and, indeed, should be repeated
every spring. Stokowski was ready. Finally we were at
the door, where Bill and Stoki shook hands flaccidly,
and Bill did say, "It was an honor to meet you, sir." (The
effect was vitiated somewhat by the fact that Bill
seemed to be addressing the compliment to the silent
singer.)

After the foregoing, I was surprised to get a call from
Stokowski about an hour later telling me that he
thought Mr. Montgomery was "a wahndafooll young
man. Remarkable." Well, who was I to judge? Bill was
sending Stokowski and the orchestra to Europe, and I
would have to agree that was "wahndafooll" enough to
make up for a century of social gracelessness, let alone
fifteen-minutes worth.

Bill established at once that we ought to have a bank
account for the tour organization, and this announcement was greeted with such a burst of unanimity as is
usually reserved for the hostess at a kiddies' party when
she asks if everyone is ready for ice cream. Bill started
the account with one thousand dollars. I was a little
disappointed at the size of this initial investment, but
was hardly in a position to make this evident. Beggars
and choosers, don't you know.

The orchestra payroll, remember, would run, approximately, for the five-week tour plus one week of rehearsals in New York, one hundred thousand dollars. Transportation would be separate and sizable. A fee of twenty-five thousand dollars was proposed for Stokowski. This was one of the times Bill evinced annoyance, the Stokowski-fee proposal being mine. "That's absurd. We have to give him at least fifty." Quickly agreed. Stokowski had gotten precious little from the many engagements he conducted with us, and who was I to gainsay this benefactor who seemed to be aiding the orchestra even retroactively? Fifty it was, and all Stokowski's.

Bill was at this time interviewing the heads of publicity and public-relations firms, for he was insistent that this tour and the long-range plans for the orchestra had to be given the widest possible exposure worldwide. Fine. I told him that he was dealing with some of the most expensive agencies in a very expensive business. He squelched me: "Hang the expense. We must have the best." He said this in a manner that would have made Farragut spurning the "torpedoes" seem positively hesitant.

Meanwhile, back at her apartment on the West Side, the "lady" was planning parties and receptions at a feverish clip and getting a gratifying number of her contacts to give soirees and teas and cocktail hours for the cause. And Bill was not refusing tangential financial assistance, despite his Olympian confidence. We were embarked on a costly venture—even he conceded that. Besides the orchestral and conductorial expenses already noted were such incidentals as shipment of instruments (with heavy insurance) and music, need for equipment men, local stage hands in the theatres and concert halls we would use abroad, and many, many etceteras. We were involved, any way we looked at it, in a quarter-of-a-million-dollar project. I used this figure over and over in my consultations with Bill. He was undeterred. "I will guarantee every penny we will need for this tour. I certify to that." He could hardly disguise his disdain for those of little faith who concerned themselves with sums.

About a month had elapsed, the first of the parties had been given (and netted a big fat two hundred dollars), Bill was intensively interviewing media bigwigs, and "the lady" was furious over the terrible potato salad one luncheon hostess had foisted on her guests, who included the world-renowned Miss Elizabeth Taylor. There is no record of what the future Mrs. Burton gave to the cause. But I looked more at the calendar than at Miss Taylor, and it showed that the departure date for the tour was less than three months away. This was a ridiculously short time for so monumental an undertaking—monumental by our lights, certainly. Despite Bill's insistence that we required "geniuses" to handle our publicity, he hadn't found the right team yet, and the first release, announcing the project, was penned by our two regular Jacks-of-all-trades, Stewart Warkow and Janice Kurtis. It got really prominent space in *The New York Times,* the most important outlet internationally, and prominent notice in papers and magazines all over the world. We always had friends and sympathizers in the various media, and despite our primitive organization, our press book was miraculous.

One immediate result of the first release was a storm of calls from musicians, from literally all over the country, asking to be included in the orchestra that would go to Europe. The regular members of the Symphony, about two-thirds of whom could go on the tour, accounted for about fifty places. This was half of what Stokowski would need. The conductor was jubilant these days. He promised such concerts as our European audiences had rarely heard before. But as we talked program, he made one decision that struck me as inappropriate. He thought that we should perform the *New World* Symphony of Dvořák on almost every program. "It is *the* symphony of America," he declared.

The *New World* is a great work, and I love it. But it is overplayed to put it mildly, and anyway, it is not really an American symphony at all; it is pure Czech nostalgia. To be sure, Dvořák composed most of the symphony in America, and it has suggestions of Indian and Negro themes here and there, but fundamentally it is a warm-hearted evocation of Bohemia, for which Dvořák longed fervently as he went around the States as a guest conductor. (His most important American post was as director of the New York Conservatory, a forerunner of Juilliard.) His letters from America—superb ones, for Dvořák was one of the most articulate of musicians—are full of affection for this country and its people, but he always returns to the subject of his homeland and his pining for it. He was happiest in the Middle West, where he sought out Czech communities and spent his most contented American hours with them singing and playing the folk songs he loved so much, and used with such marvelous effect in the great Slavonic dances. There is a touching description of a picnic in Omaha, where some farmers organized a band for him and played Bohemian music. He says this moved him as much as any musical experience he ever had. The title page of the E Minor Symphony has the words, inscribed at the last minute, *"Z nového světa"* ("From the New World"). He explained in letters and articles that all he intended were some feelings evoked in him by America. But he makes absolutely clear that it was not an American symphony. He rued the inscription, writing, "It seems that I have got them all confused. This is my music. It is of my home, and at home they will understand what I meant." Home was Bohemia.

I told some of this to Stokowski, marveling at my own effrontery, and he heard me out. He then said, "We must play the Dvořák. It is such an American symphony."

I suppose my exposition of why I thought he should reconsider making the *New World* the basic piece in our repertoire smacked of musicology, and Stoki sneered at musicologists. His ultimate reproach to anyone who bored him with musical talk was, "He sounds like a musicologist." Yet the conductor did indulge in a free-wheeling kind of musicology himself. When I was a boy in Philadelphia, I heard Stoki on a few occasions talk about the shame of society, past and present, not providing for the financial needs of some of the great masters. He would always end by saying that it was horrible that Bach had been buried in a pauper's grave. Over and over, critics, not especially erudite ones, would take issue with this uncorroborated fact. No Spitta myself, I have read enough to know that while old Johann Sebastian was a long way from well-to-do, he was never a pauper. He often had to engage in humiliating musical occupations and was never treated in his time with the deference due one of the greatest geniuses that ever lived. He didn't even get a job with the Margrave of

Brandenburg, although that worthy got six pretty good concertos for his money. But he wasn't a pauper, and his burial was adequate by lower middle-class eighteenth-century standards. But Stoki was still saying as late as the sixties—the curtain speech changed very little in thirty years—that Bach was laid in a pauper's grave, and we should all be ashamed of ourselves. W. A. Mozart, who was treated barbarously and whose unmarked grave was lost in a snowstorm the day after his funeral, was never mentioned by Stokowski in his speeches. I'm sure he knew about him. But Bach was always Stoki's "Exhibit A" to demonstrate callousness in the business of music.

Well, whatever Dvořák had thought, his "American" symphony was set for performance. I did have joyful moments with Stoki. He promised to take me to some of the greatest restaurants in the world as we made our triumphant progress through the Old World. He listed the restaurants, and I all but salivated in anticipation. One thing was certain: Stoki had been around. He took no interest in the logistic preparations, except for constantly urging us to get the best available players, which was fair enough. He would carry this desire a little too far at times by getting in touch with eminent first players of other orchestras, including some veterans of his Philadelphia days, and informing them that Mr. Toobeen would fix it with their conductors for them to miss the end of their own orchestra's regular season. I didn't do it. I can imagine the reaction of Mr. Ormandy, never rumored to be a bosom friend of Stoki's, when I made that Stokowskian request. But Stoki was absolutely correct in pushing for a great orchestra.

Sol Hurok, a great man with a phrase even if his syntax was not always reminiscent of Addison or Steele, once said, "I don't like it when the only thing that is happening is nothing." And despite the interviews, and the parties, and the languor and the hauteur, the only thing that was really happening with Bill Montgomery was nothing. Only a dribble of money was coming in from the New York activities, and the commitment was such that it was certain that Bill would have to come up with two hundred fifty thousand dollars if the tour was to proceed. Somehow the six-digit number sounded less than the imperial phrase "a quarter of a million"—but, however you said it, that's what we needed.

The personnel manager, the poor unfortunate who is responsible for negotiating with the individual musicians—he is also known in musical business circles as the contractor—was on the verge of collapse. He had about eighty-five players on a "hold" basis, which meant they were reserving the dates, but there was nothing binding on either side. This whole matter was under the control of the musicians' union because once the musician is hired, the contractor is responsible for the full amount of the time contracted for. If a man were to be hired for the five weeks of the tour plus the one week of rehearsals in New York, the contractor, and by extension the Symphony of the Air, would owe him the union rate for the whole engagement. This meant at least one thousand dollars per man. Eighty-five men were being held pending the final act of hiring, and the concomitant liability of the orchestra; twenty-five were still to be chosen. The personnel man was being hounded by the musicians, and with good reason. They were not taking other engagements for the six-week period and stood to lose a great deal of money if for any reason the trip did not take place. Union regulations provided that men could be disengaged up to two weeks before an engagement, but this was not applicable in the tour dealings. There were no secrets from the union, and until the monies for the men were posted in escrow with the treasurer of Local 802, there would be no hiring, and once the union got the money, you could bet there would be no disengagements.

Musicians are spectacular hounders in the best of times, as are all underpaid workers when their modest incomes are in jeopardy. I must confess, however, that sympathetic as I was to the musician in the ranks, I myself had an unlisted telephone number. In addition to their justifiable complaints, of which there were many, the musicians also used my wire as a forum for discussions of conductors' inadequacies, questions on how the future for the orchestra *really* looked, and attempts to have me intervene with the personnel manager to let them out of the rehearsal of the Haydn *Creation* because they had a chance to do a Duz commercial. I knew very well that helping to sell the detergent paid five times as much as *The Creation*. I got unlisted, however, when a viola player of great musical skill but less intellectual stature called me at 3:30 a.m. to make sure where a rehearsal two weeks off was being held. This was not the first time. I figured *some* things could wait for regular office hours. The officials of the orchestra and, come to think of it, anybody that wanted it soon had the secret number. My deepest sympathy was reserved for the personnel manager, for all the aforementioned reasons.

The departure date was now about two months off. Every time I attempted to talk to Bill about the urgency of posting the money with the union as the required guarantee for engaging the men, he said, "I'll take care of that any day now," in a just barely impatient tone.

Once, when I asked Bill about his writing, he didn't respond, but did say, "I'm an artist. I hate material things. But God was good to my daddy, and I've had all the money I've ever needed. Now I can do God's work with this orchestra." I accepted this sanctity, and I desisted from asking him that if he was an artist, what beside the *Atlantic* piece there was in his canon. But if we were to carry God's work forward, we had better get to the material things Bill hated—and quick. Bill at one party called the proposed tour a "musical crusade." He emphasized dramatically that it would end in the Vatican. Now this was reversing the direction of the *other* crusades, and I couldn't help thinking there were a great many indications that this was a crusade in reverse. Anyway, I had read Voltaire on crusades, and they were pretty material—Bill might have hated the real thing.

Now the top brass of the union began to call me daily, sometimes twice. Every little chat with one of the executives of 802 began in the same limpid manner: "Toobin. What the hell's going on over there. The men are out of their minds. And I think you are going to wind up in the booby hatch." One more mod official suggested the "funny farm." But it was clear that they were confident of my eventual incarceration for psychiatric reasons.

When, finally, the president of the union himself called me, a rare distinction, I asked him why the constant harping on my sanity, because that august being had, in the course of asking me where the money was, also alluded to my imminent trip to the "booby hatch." He said he thought I was a "nice Jewish fellow," reasonably bright, but "only a lunatic would try to run a symphony without money." He said he was aware of what we were trying to do, he worshipped Toscanini, and he even admired the courage shown. "But," he concluded gloomily, "enough's enough. You can't run a symphony orchestra without money."

It's never been said better or more clearly. You *can't* run a symphony orchestra without money. Desire, ideals, artistic ambition, resourcefulness, courage, determination, even some quixotism are virtues, I think. But in America, in my time, art is a commodity, and not enough people want to buy it. Somebody or something —like a government—has to subsidize it. Or it can't live. "You can't run a symphony orchestra without money."

The crisis with Bill was precipitated one day when he called to ask me if I thought it was a good idea to get Beniamino Gigli to sing the Italian anthem and "The Star-Spangled Banner" at the Vatican concert. I didn't, because the great tenor had died three years before. Unruffled, he continued, "Well what about Pinza?" Same problem. Dead three years. Bill pressed on, "Huh —well, who else?" It was here that I exploded.

Up to then, I had been a human battlefield, with contending armies trying to get me to either force the hand of Bill, or not to force the hand of Bill, because if he gets angry and disgusted and walks out, where will we be then? I was torn by both forces, a veritable Gettysburg of Fifty-seventh Street. Now I exploded.

"I don't know who else, goddamn it. But I know we better get some goddamned money into the union and hire some musicians or we have to announce a cancellation because the president of the tour organization couldn't raise the money he promised. This is it, Bill." Fine original phrase that!

Short silence on the other end. Then the usual patient, condescending tone. It was a sarcastic purr. "Oh, I kind of thought something was bothering you. You seemed edgy lately." Then, more firmly and with dramatic effect: "I shall deposit two hundred thousand dollars in the Chase Manhattan Bank one week from today. I've worked everything out. The tour goes forward."

It was a Thursday when Bill announced to me the date of the posting of the monies. We had to live until another Thursday rolled around. It was going to be a long week, but at least we had something to point to. The men were informed that the happy ending was in sight. I had told Stokowski about the problems with Bill, but he stayed serene. He continued to assure me that Mr. Montgomery was "a fine person," and that if he gave his word that he would finance the tour, it would be so. We discussed Bill briefly, and I told Stokowski that Bill reminded me of one of Scott Fitzgerald's rich boys. Throughout the nerve-wracking negotiations, his aloof, supercilious manner, his patent refusal to be pinned down by the practical, and even his appearance had brought Fitzgerald's characters to mind.

Stoki said, "Who is this Fitzgerald?"

I answered, thinking he hadn't heard correctly, "Scott Fitzgerald—you know the novelist. Gatsby."

Stoki looked blank, as blank as one with his hooded, hawk eyes could look. "I don't know him. Is he good? Write his name down and bring me a list of his books. I'll try to find time to read them."

Stoki wasn't the man for put-ons generally; his humor, what there was of it, didn't lie in that direction. Had he really never heard of F. Scott Fitzgerald? At any rate, he had complete confidence in Bill Montgomery, and when I told him that the money for the tour would be in our hands in a week, according to Bill, Stoki said, in essence, "I told you so."

Bill called the day after the historic announcement to say that the "lady" was going to invite the governor and the mayor to come to the airport to see the orchestra off. I said I was glad. Then I didn't hear from him, but he went to a party on Monday night. There was nothing unusual. In recent weeks he had taken to calling me rarely. But I *was* pretty edgy.

The week passed. I will not bother to discuss the anxieties as it drew closer to Thursday. *Der Tag* arrived. I heard nothing from Bill. At 2:00 p.m., having skipped lunch for fear of missing Bill's call, I called his apartment. No answer. This in itself was not significant because he was almost never there and had no answering service. I called the "lady," and she had heard nothing from him. She sounded a little apprehensive, but then she always sounded that way on the telephone, since hers was obviously an unsettled economic existence. We used to get many calls from credit managers seeking out the "lady," who gave us as a business reference, thereby showing the paucity of her resources. But the day was passing, and there was no call from Bill. I personally placed the last call to his apartment at 2:00 a.m. the next morning. I let it ring a long time. No one answered.

Friday morning I decided to call Bill Montgomery's father in North Carolina. We had never spoken, and except for an allusion here and there to the divine intercession which had made them rich, Bill never talked

about his father. His mother he had never mentioned.
Or anyone back in North Carolina, except our honorary
chairman, Senator Sam. We placed a call to the Montgomery textile plant, and in a very short time William
Montgomery, Sr., was on the line. He greeted me cordially, making sure of the spelling of my name. I told
him, in very condensed form, what the problem was, but
I felt he already knew all about it.

When I paused, he said, "You mean you all got involved in a *business* matter with Bill? [The word "business" was pronounced with heavy and ironic emphasis.]
Why, my goodness, you seem to have an important position, and I don't understand. You and all those other
folks. Getting involved with Bill."

I told him about the committee Bill had raised, and
the celebrities and world-prominent people who had
written to him, personally, pledging their assistance.
Montgomery, Sr., interrupted: "But they didn't pledge
any money, did they? Assistance!" I continued, describing the reams of publicity, the coast-to-coast clippings,
the many articles. In all this publicity it was clearly
stated that William Montgomery, Jr., was president of
the tour organization. Hadn't he known about all this,
hadn't he seen any of the publicity?

"Certainly," he snapped. "But I didn't ask him to do it.
I didn't ask him to do anything! And all you folks up
there—even the Cardinal—getting mixed up with Bill."

Well, there we all were, the celebrities, Senator Sam,
the Cardinal, all the musicians—all dupes. Where was
Bill, and would his daddy help us? Mr. Montgomery
said, "Let me wait until Monday morning and see if I
hear from Bill. I think I will, because he always comes
running to me when he's in it. Call me on Monday and

I'll see what we can do." Bill was in it. We were all in it.

Monday morning at 9:00 a.m. I received a call from a New York attorney, member of a very prominent firm, who said he represented Mr. William Montgomery, Sr. He asked to see me and the Symphony's lawyer that afternoon at 2:00 p.m. We went, taking along the personnel manager, another official of the orchestra, and Stu Warkow. We arrived, and the lawyer came out to the reception desk and ushered us in. At a chair beside his desk sat Bill Montgomery. He barely glanced at us, and looked only at the lawyer throughout the meeting, the way he did with the silent singer. But the silent singer wasn't here this time.

The lawyer began by saying that his client, Mr. Montgomery, Sr., was very sorry about the "confusion." He continued, "Mr. Montgomery will arrive at Teterboro Airport tonight at seven. He will talk to Bill, and he is ready to assume all of Bill's obligations for this tour."

We didn't say much. We were in a state of shock, I suppose. I did wonder about Teterboro Airport. I just wasn't privy to the ways of the rich. My lawyer told me, when I whispered a query about it, that Teterboro was where the private planes land. I should not include our lawyer, a very suave and competent gentleman named Clifton Stannage, in the shock syndrome. He began to try to work things out immediately. He explained the enormous union pressures on us, and the time problems, which, with the tour about two months off, were terrific. He urged that the very first order of business be the placing of the necessary monies in escrow with the union so that the orchestra could be engaged. The lawyer listened attentively; Bill looked right at the lawyer, but I couldn't help noticing that whenever Mr. Stannage would press the point of the money being in the union's hands as soon as possible, Bill would faintly, but definitely, sneer. He was still looking very much *au-dessus de la bataille.*

Montgomery's lawyer said all would be well, Mr. Montgomery would be in New York for a few days to settle everything, and concluded, "Mr. Montgomery is sorry for your trouble, and after he talks to Bill, he will make good on all Bill's obligations."

My mind stopped at the lawyer's second reference to "talking to Bill" (as it had at the first), but I blocked out everything but the euphoria that we were going on the trip after all, and the idea that maybe, sometimes, somewhere, justice conquers. Given that this was justice. I thought it was.

The next morning Mr. Montgomery called me at home at 8:00 a.m., before I could get to the office. "I spoke to Bill. I told him I will deposit the money you need anywhere you say this morning. But he has to leave with me for the Menninger Clinic this afternoon. There's no other way. He said he'll think it over, and I'll call you back as soon as I know. He has to go to the Menninger, or I have to teach him a lesson. [Teach *him* a lesson?] Otherwise he'll keep hurting people like you and that woman in the museum in San Francisco and that poor opera man in Chicago. Bill needs a doctor. Or else I'm determined to teach him a lesson by letting this orchestra tour die. And he'll know it's his fault. Maybe that will wake him up."

There is not much more to tell. Montgomery's lawyer called that afternoon at three to say that the Montgomerys had flown back to North Carolina together to talk it all out. They would try to be in touch with me "soon." The lawyer could not or would not tell me any more. I called the personnel manager and the union. The "hold" was taken off the musicians, and they were told that the tour was almost certainly cancelled. They should by all means avail themselves of whatever employment they could get during the "tour" period. Everyone was more understanding than I thought they would be. Maybe they had given up a long time before and were just going through the motions of pressuring me. I don't know. In a few weeks we got a lovely letter from a papal secretary saying he was very sorry that our tour was cancelled due to Mr. Montgomery's illness. He sent the pope's greeting and blessing, and added that the Holy Father felt that ours is the good life, the happy life, because to make music is "one of mankind's highest callings."

Stokowski was the most difficult of the principals. He wanted to know if I had Bill's address so that his manager could contact him about paying Stokowski "for the time he had wasted." The conductor said he had given up "many, many engagements all over the world." He was positively frosty with me, giving me a deep look out of the chicken-hawk eyes and saying I should be more careful when bringing him projects in the future. As I was leaving, I said I had written down the names of some Fitzgerald novels for him. He said he wouldn't have time to read them.

I never heard about Bill Montgomery again. The "lady," her unconquerable confidence shaken, left the music world, and I bumped into her at a sculptor's opening some time later. We just exchanged greetings. And to this day I wonder what it was Bill did to the lady in the museum in San Francisco and that poor opera man in Chicago. I wish we could all get together some time.

♪

When the Symphony was about to expire, there was one last encounter with a bizarre representative of the wealthy that bears telling, if only as a warning against being taken in by names. We will call this fellow George Wentworth, though his real name is a household word for riches. In fact, he is the descendant of one of those lines with intermarriages in which *everybody's* name means money. He lived very well and talked a superlative game. But I have no idea how much his family *trusted* him with. I met him at a party peopled with television folk, George then being a public-relations man for one of the networks. And he had one thing in common with Bill Montgomery: he was carrying around a magazine article which he had written. This piece, about serious music on the West Coast, had been published about a year before the time I met him in a mass-circulation weekly. I had apparently missed it when it came out. So naturally we had something to talk about.

George Wentworth was huge: six feet five, about two hundred fifty pounds, looking not unlike pictures of Thomas Wolfe. He could easily have written his serious-music article on top of a refrigerator. I skimmed the article as we sat amid the forced gaiety of a typical media affair—this one was a brunch on New Year's Day. Though the piece was a lot longer than Bill Montgomery's opus, it seemed equally forgettable. But George was very enthusiastic about the Symphony of the Air, although it was obvious he didn't know anything about it except for the Toscanini association. We talked about current orchestral affairs, and I told him about a development that had taken place just a day or so before. This might have been a mistake, but I was so tired of lamentations that I had difficulty containing even potential good news. It was rare.

The tidings I had for Wentworth were certainly important. They involved two violinists: one, a world-famous virtuoso, who loved to dabble in the politics of art, and was making some efforts to help us; the other, Jack Benny.

For a period of years Benny had been appearing on benefit concerts to help symphony orchestras all over the country. He had raised a considerable amount of money. Now, his emissary, the virtuoso, said it was our turn. It was good news that couldn't have come at a more opportune time. I told George the bare facts of Benny's offer, and he shrieked with excitement. In fact, he startled one hors d'oeuvres-carrying maid into dropping her tray into the lap of a famous news correspondent. Wentworth's excitement was caused, he said, by the great coincidence of his father and stepmother being great friends of the comedian. His stepmother, now deceased, had been a famous singer, whose marriage into the financial empire of George's family was front-page news, although it was greeted by the Wentworths with less than unrestrained joy. He asked if he could take me to see Benny when he came to New York, "because we're very close." I think my temptation was legitimate: a personal tie with Benny, and through one of the imperial names of American finance. I told him that as a matter of fact I had an appointment with Benny in a few days, and I would be delighted to have him along. So George Wentworth and I went to see Jack Benny in his suite at the Pierre. Jack, nervously pacing around the large living room in his dressing gown, complaining about his digestion, had the famous harried look that his fans know so well. He had a cold, too; he missed California; in short, he wasn't being at all funny. But he had a very exciting double project for the Symphony.

First, he would do a benefit concert with the orchestra. It would consist of his usual routine—playing in his inimitable manner, arguing fine points with the conductor, displacing the concert master, and so forth. I thought his musical act hilarious and in good taste. In addition, there was an even bigger plan. Benny had composed a kind of comic concerto for violin and orchestra. It was filled with imaginative touches and evidenced real musical acumen. Best of all, a major record company had told Benny it wanted to record it, and Jack said we could accomplish this in New York around the time of his concert with us. Finally, he was talking to his television sponsor about the possibility of doing the "concerto" on one of his TV specials. It sounded like a bonanza for us.

But as he told us the good news, he continued to be in a gloomy mood. He was especially nervous and serious about his composition. When he told us about some of the business in the "concerto," it sounded hilarious, and I laughed. Wrong reaction. It seemed to disconcert him, and he told me to "get serious." This was no time to be fooling around. I thought at once of the Bert Lahr story which E. Y. Harburg, the lyricist, had told me. Lahr went to that gentleman and described a wonderfully zany scene. The lyricist broke up. Lahr, looking hurt, said, "You can laugh, but that's funny." Benny likewise expected a sober reaction to his antics.

George sat through the meeting with a constant broad grin on his big face. Benny hadn't greeted him with any particular enthusiasm, but as I have stated, the comedian seemed to be in a very dour state. He did remember George's stepmother fondly and asked to be remembered to his father.

But when Jack had finished his exposition, George took over. He said, "I think there's a million dollars in this for the orchestra." Jack just looked glum. George said further that he would like to be the liaison between Jack and the orchestra, because "we are friends."

Jack still looked glum. He said, "I don't give a damn how you work it out. Just stay in touch. There's a hell of a lot of work to do, especially with the 'concerto.' Just stay in touch. I'm leaving for the Carribean next week. I'm going to play some clubs and get some sun. Maybe I'll lose this goddamned cold New York gave me. I'll leave you my whole itinerary. Just stay in touch."

George assured him he would stay in touch; I assured him George would stay in touch. We were going to stay in touch. Jack walked gloomily down the hall with us to the elevator, and suddenly "eeked" as I had heard him do so many times for so many years on radio and television. "Eek! I'm walking around in my pajamas." He had apparently somewhere along the line discarded his dressing gown, and none of us had noticed it.

So Jack left for warmer climes, and George settled down to staying in touch. Benny would be gone for about eight weeks, and after that we would get together to set the dates for the concert, the recording, and, with good luck, the telecast. The latter two meant really significant money for the musicians, and together they all might pay a substantial number of bills.

Every few days I would talk to George about matters in general, although all I cared to hear about was how he was doing with Jack Benny. George, though, was now a global planner on my staff, his vision all-encompassing. I tuned out when he talked about a tour to Europe [!], but I listened when he said his father was going to approach Judy Garland about a benefit for the orchestra. As for Jack, when I asked what was going on, George would bray loudly, one of his less charming mannerisms, and say, over and over, "What a character." George was given to brays and guffaws, and his largeness made him seem—well, not like the Harvard graduate he was. But everything was fine with Jack; he gave no details, actually, and we didn't really need any until his return. Jack just wanted to talk over his music, and George was our resident "stay-in-toucher." The day after George reported a conversation with Jack in Antigua and said that Jack was chafing at the bit to get back so that we could work harder on getting the telecast, I received a chilling telephone call from the virtuoso violinist who had brought us Benny.

It began, "What the hell is the matter with you."

This was a not unfamiliar greeting, and forgetting for a moment whom I was talking to, I was about to say, by reflex, "There will be a check in the mail tomorrow morning," when I came to. "What's wrong?" I asked, really baffled. We didn't owe *him* any money.

"What's wrong? Two months ago you went to see Jack Benny. And you took that polar-bear Wentworth along, God knows why. He told Jack he would be in touch with him, right? Well, that —— [and this time he called him not a polar bear, but the Yiddish noun for a special, phallic kind of dolt] *never* got in touch with Jack. Never.

Not once. And Jack is madder than I ever knew him to be in my whole life. Can you imagine? A sweet guy like Jack, and your — [see above] doesn't bother to call him for three months."

The Benny project died at the hands of the affluent Mr. Wentworth. Benny wouldn't even talk with me.

I finish this section on money-raising much the same as I started it (back in the Freud room with Bernays), pleading my ignorance of psychoanalytic lore. How could George Wentworth so deceive us? How could he have repeated conversations verbatim that never took place? When I confronted him, how could he have said, "It's complicated, and I'll discuss it with you at length, but I can't now"? There are more things, Horatio, but why did they keep happening to me? The fact is that the arts attract a lunatic fringe as does politics and other serious pursuits. Some rich dilettantes, when they are not clinical cases like the Bills and the Georges, are careless people. Scott Fitzgerald in that marvelous scene in *Gatsby* has Nick Carraway consciously avoid Daisy and Tom Buchanan because he wants to avert the damage they have already done to so many people, good and bad. His ultimate denigration of them is that they are "careless people."

"You can't run a symphony orchestra without money." But as you cut through the underbrush that is the moneyed world of New York society, you don't always have a chance to avoid the Toms and Daisys. You think maybe this time it will be different, maybe this time they won't be careless. But it never happened to me.

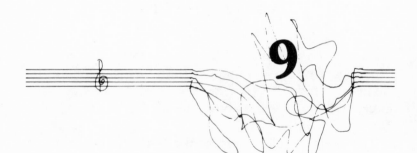

We were rehearsing for a concert with Stokowski in one of the ramshackle rehearsal halls of the New York City Center when I was called to the telephone. It was January 16, 1957. I was informed that Arturo Toscanini had died in his Riverdale home; he was two months shy of his ninetieth year. I immediately interrupted the rehearsal to inform Stokowski (he pursed his lips, but said nothing) and then made a short announcement to the men. There were before me quite a few who had been with the NBC Symphony from its inception in 1937, and even some who had played for Maestro in the Philharmonic. One—the English-horn player Filippo Ghignatti—had played under him as far back as the 1920s in the La Scala orchestra. And there were some very young players who had never even seen Toscanini conduct. Stokowski asked if we should continue the rehearsal, and I took it on myself to say that we should.

Toscanini had always said that death was never to interfere with life—indeed, despite his great age, he was loath to talk about it, and his intimates reported that he scorned anything connected with it, but arrogantly, as though it weren't worth much thought. As a result, he hated bouquets of flowers, which, after an unfortunate scene following his first concert with NBC on Christmas night 1937, he was never given. As the tremendous ovation rolled over Studio 8-H at the conclusion of Maestro's performance of the Brahms First, an NBC page, so instructed, moved down the aisle and handed Toscanini a huge bouquet. Toscanini took the flowers, walked briskly off stage, and dashed the bouquet to the ground the second he was in the wings. *"Stupido!"* he shouted, so that he could easily be heard in the first rows. "Is for funeral! *Vergogna!* Nobawdy here dies!"

So I felt no qualms about asking Stokowski to continue with the rehearsal, and the men later approved my action. By the time the rehearsal ended, an hour or so later, there were already press and television on hand to talk with some of the players and, far less important, with me. The CBS reporter was the now eminent Harry Reasoner, and I remember telling him that Toscanini had always been both contemptuous of and somewhat disoriented by death. I was told by his son, Walter, that he would visit Verdi's grave and weep, saying, *"Povero Verdi, è morto, è morto"*—this despite the fact that if that great composer had been still alive he would have been in the neighborhood of one hundred seventeen. Toscanini was also superstitious about death, confiding to some friends, as he grew very old, that he was certain to die at eighty-seven—the same age as Verdi did. And this would be fitting, since Verdi had been from first to last his idol and inspiration. (There is some mystery as to whether or not he was ever told of Cantelli's death, most people who went to Riverdale to see the Maestro or his family having been told that as far as Toscanini knew, Cantelli was ill, and his return to America had been delayed for that reason. But many said, knowingly, that he knew all right and that he was suffering terribly from that knowledge.) Above all he was not working and this was already death.

Now the Maestro was gone, and we who were trying desperately to save his orchestra from what seemed—and was—certain economic strangulation thought that a real tribute to him would be to make his passing of help to the group. Therefore, in consultation with the board of the orchestra, at that time made up of real Toscanini veterans who had played under him through most of his tenure at NBC, I began to plan a memorial concert.

We proposed to have three of the great conductors of the world lead a program of music connected in some aesthetic or personal way with Toscanini. By a combination of good luck—their availability—and their desire to honor the great conductor, we engaged Bruno Walter, Pierre Monteux, (with Maestro's passing the dean of conductors), and Charles Munch, a friend of Toscanini's and a conductor he admired greatly. There weren't many such. I talked program with them, and we decided that Walter would do the *Eroica;* Munch would do Debussy's *La Mer,* a masterpiece which Toscanini did in such a unique incandescent and dramatic manner as to make his reading almost a separate art form of its own; and Monteux agreed to abide by a whim of mine, but anyone who heard that concert will agree that it was well that he did so. Toscanini had always performed and loved the *Enigma* Variations of Edward Elgar, a set in which Elgar described his circle of friends with tenderness, passion, and humor. The music, while at best a minor masterpiece, is still so warm and in some strange way so personal and intimate that I felt it would close the program on a dignified note worthy of Toscanini. Monteux's superb performance vindicated the choice. But the scheduling of this great event was only the beginning; much was to occur between the arrangement of the memorial concert and the moment when Bruno Walter would bring his baton down on those two stupendous chords which open Beethoven's heroic symphony.

The day all arrangements were completed for the three conductors, I was at my desk, surrounded by board members, and we were trying to work out a price scale that would get people to come and make us rich at the same time—or at least let us pay some of our bills. Now there came that harbinger of the future, the telephone buzzer: David Oppenheimer of Columbia Records wanted me. I was already furious—my normal state—since in my usual anticipation of nothing but harassment, I was sure he was going to ask for free tickets to the gala. Like the man in the famous "borrowing-the-jack" story, I was about to tell him off violently when he made a mild inquiry. Would I be in my office for the next few minutes? Assured that I would be, he said that Goddard Lieberson would call me soon. This was typical of the protocol surrounding a communication from one of the mighty. Heaven forfend that the head of Columbia Records should call and I be out. Better some aide-de-camp waste his less momentously precious time. Anyway, Lieberson called in about five minutes, but there was still awesome preparation under way. Lieberson asked if I would be in my office for a while, because Wanda Toscanini Horowitz wanted to talk to me. This, however, was genuinely exciting news, since the Toscanini family had never been close to the Symphony at all, and now in the immediate aftermath of Maestro's death this call held promise. Mrs. Horowitz telephoned almost the second Lieberson hung up.

"My husban'—you know, Volodye—would like to do something for Father." Sounds simple, that sentence. But my mind reeled at the implications of it. I immediately understood that her husband, Vladimir Horowitz —"you know, Volodye"—possibly the greatest pianist who ever lived, was going to play again in tribute to his father-in-law. It must be remembered that at this time Horowitz had not played in public for many years, and one of the great questions of the music world was whether or not he ever would again. He was, among other things, probably the biggest gate attraction in the music world of our time.

Mrs. Horowitz continued, "Volodye would like to play Brahms B Flat Concerto with your orchestra, if you would be good enough to arrange a concert. I just spoke to Bruno Walter, and he says he will conduct. So, what do you say?"

I didn't faint; I didn't collapse. I was far too deeply in debt to indulge such romantic reactions. I did shake a lot. In short, I said I would be good enough. We discussed a date in May, she said I should rent Carnegie Hall right away, and she asked two other things. First she asked if I could get Frank Miller, the fine first cellist of the NBC and a great Toscanini favorite, to play in the concert, since "Volodye loves how he plays the solo in the slow movement." (If you've ever heard the great Toscanini-Horowitz recording of the Brahms B Flat, you'll know why.) Miller was at this time the resident conductor of the orchestra in Orlando, Florida, and I had no idea if he could make it or not. But I said, of course, I

would get Miller, and at that moment I would have trot-
ted down to Orlando and *carried* Miller back by myself.
Piggyback. The second question was not that easy.

"I know you are giving this concert with three conductors [as in the usual manner of secrets in the music
business, the word of the three-conductor concert was
all over the Fifty-seventh street area before I was off the
phone with the assorted maestri]. Do me a favor. Bruno
Walter is very busy, and old, and he wants so much to
do this concert with Volodye. Let him out of the concert
with the other conductors." And not stopping to even let
me consider this serious suggestion, she continued,
"Who can we get in his place?"

Well, *we* were already looking for a replacement for
Walter, in one second. So after all my years of Tos-
canini-worship, his daughter and I were *we*, allies,
confidants. The little boy in me, a constant threat to and
antagonist of the man supposedly maturing through the
years, loved it. And I acquiesced immediately. "Of
course, Mrs. Horowitz, if that is what you and your husband and Dr. Walter want, we'll work something out."
She pressed me, however.

"But who can we get for the three-conductor concert?"
Again the ego-inflating "we."

I had a thought right away. "How about Reiner?" I
admired Fritz Reiner as a conductor, even though I realized that he was a uniquely bad tempered, cruel man
who had sent plenty of musicians into rest homes and
onto analysts' couches.

There was a very short silence, and she said, "O.K. Not
a bad idea. Let's get Reiner." One last sweet term of
association with a Toscanini: "Let's." Let us. Me and
Wanda.

This was a moment to savor and I savored it. One concert with three of the great conductors of the world; one concert featuring the return from self-imposed exile of one of the musical giants of history. And such certain fringe benefits as sure recordings, radio and TV possibilities, oceans of publicity, and above all gate receipts that would bale me out for—well, for a while anyway. But nothing comes simple in the business of music, and this was a towering peak in the range of my agonies.

"We" then proceeded to get Reiner. I called Walter Prude at the Hurok office and told him my story. Prude is the prince of the management business, an urbane, intelligent, sensitive man of exquisite taste in literature and music, a tennis player one step from tournament caliber; in short, a puzzle, the puzzle being what is he doing in the music business, as a manager yet, and the very best. But miserable jungle of cutthroat mores that it is, it does attract a surprising number of good people —all of them, I suppose, resolved to change the jungle into a garden, and failing.

Prude said he would call Reiner, and for God's sake not to let him get wind of the fact that he was second choice (really fourth choice). He called back, chuckling, saying Reiner had been his usual warm, charming self, his grunts having apparently indicated that he would do the concert. He would conduct the *Eroica,* the piece Walter had chosen. Told there would be no fee, since the concert was to help the Symphony of the Air, he snorted but made one odd condition: he would have to be brought to the concert from Westport, Connecticut, where he lived, in a taxicab. I asked Prude if it had to be a taxicab; how about a private car, maybe even a limousine, although I cringed, knowing how expensive it was to bring Stokowski from Eighty-seventh Street and Fifth Avenue to Carnegie Hall in a chauffeured limousine.

"Look," said Prude, sagaciously as always, "don't fool around with Reiner. He's doing it without a fee, and he probably thinks he should be doing the whole concert instead of sharing it with two others. So if he says a taxi, get him there in a taxi. You drive it, if necessary." (This, plus carrying Frank Miller from Orlando, gave me a pretty full transportation schedule for the concert.)

And so Reiner was engaged. At 1:00 p.m. At 8:30 p.m., things changed. I was at Carnegie Hall, where we were giving a concert with Sir Thomas Beecham. I was distraught by at least two things at this event: 1) Beecham's gout had been acting up, and his wife, the latest, a lovely, willowy thing about fifty years his junior, assured me, "Oh, Sir Thomas will certainly get through the first half"; and 2) the hall was half empty. We had gambled and were giving two concerts with Beecham that week, this one on a Wednesday night and another the next Sunday. The Sunday concert sold out right away, but the one at hand was a disaster. We hoped to the very last that ticket sales would pick up and so made no provision for papering the house. Didn't happen. Stretches of empty seats in all sections. To add to my good humor, I was accosted by a well-known music critic, magazine division, who, in addition to being the most unpleasant single character I ever had anything to do with in the music business, was also a friend of Beecham's.

"C'm'ere," he snarled as soon as he saw me. (Note the deference and decorum with which I was treated by this

elder statesman of the critical fraternity.) "Where the
hell is the audience?" Now I would have loved to tell
him that it was next door at the Russian Tea Room
finishing its blini and sour cream, but I knew wherever
it was, it wasn't coming to Carnegie that night. "Christ,"
the guardian of the muses continued, "what the hell is
the old man going to think? Shit. You never do anything
right." He may have been right, I daresay, for one of the
things I did was pay him to write the program notes for
the concerts, and not a bad sum, either. Good name on
the program, said my advisers. Gives you éclat. "Shit,"
said the critic, as two young lady ushers looked around
in mild surprise, "what are we going to tell the old
man?" "We," again, this time doing nothing whatever
for my ego. The old man didn't ask, or didn't notice, and
gave a fairly competent concert considering he refused
to rehearse for more than an hour at each of the three
two-and-a-half-hour rehearsals, with possible overtime, we had contracted for. He did lead a touching,
simple elegy for Toscanini, the wistful "Last Spring" by
Grieg. It was a tasteful relief after the endless Siegfried's Funeral Marches which most orchestras were
playing to memorialize the Maestro.

But moments after the gracious critic had finished
torturing me, my assistant, Stewart Warkow, destined to
be one of the great administrators of the music business,
then just a very young kid getting experience and very
little else with the Symphony, told me that Mrs. Horowitz had to talk to me right away, and that I should call
her. Assuming the worst, I figured that Volodye had
changed his mind and that "we" were now going to look
for another pianist. I sagged—me with my gout-ridden
baronet, my half-empty house, my spluttering music

critic, and now my vanishing Volodye—I just sagged.
And I set out to call Mrs. H. once the concert was safely
launched.

Mrs. H. was pretty down herself. "We have a problem," she began. "I think I was not clear about Bruno
Walter. I spoke to him in Chicago about the concert, and
I think he wants to conduct both the three-conductor
concert and the one with Volodye. Anyway, while we
were talking, the connection was broken, and I'm not
sure where we left it." No sleuthing was necessary to
conclude that the usually benign and philosophic Viennese had hung up on my partner in the memorial plans.
"Please," Mrs. H. concluded, "could you call up Bruno
Walter and straighten things out for us?"

She helpfully gave me the number of Walter's hotel in
Chicago and was gone. I sat at the desk of the house
manager at the rear entrance to Carnegie and wished I
had followed an old teacher's advice: "Do anything, but
don't get tied up with artists. Not in a business way.
Never." I sat there because I felt sure that if I emerged
the first thing I would encounter would be my crony, the
music critic, informing me that Beecham had collapsed
of the gout, and where the hell was I whenever I was
needed? Or something nice like that. But all I heard was
the last movement of the obviously underrehearsed performance of the finale of the Beethoven Fourth—a very
tricky movement. Before I return to the horrors of the
Walter crisis (even retroactively I'm stalling), I must
add another word about the critic and the concert-at-
hand.

At the first rehearsal, Beecham, at least not superficially in any kind of physical discomfort, and I'm told
nobody can even superficially ignore the anguish of the

gout, had dismissed the orchestra early with a few hearty words: "Good morning, gentlemen, go out and have some nice lunch. For heaven sakes, don't eat goddamned hamburgers. Damned stuff kills more Americans than motor cars." At the second rehearsal he again sent the orchestra about its business, after an hour, this time without any warnings even about the dangers of hamburger consumption.

Alarmed by the protestations of the men that the program, which included, beside the Beethoven, a long Beecham-Handel piece, some Delius, and a Haydn symphony (it was a *long* program), was being inadequately prepared, I called the critic and made an appointment to see him that afternoon at the magazine to which he contributed. He was also a record reviewer, and when I came into his office a record of a Beethoven sonata was on a little portable record player by his desk, and he was writing, I could see by snooping, something about the City Center Opera. He growled a greeting, if you can call it that, and asked "What's up?" I told him the problems with Beecham's rehearsing. He listened with his usual look of pained boredom and when I had finished, in a most uncharacteristic manner, chuckled. "Jesus," he said. "Typical British contempt for audiences. He figures they don't know the difference anyway, so why kill yourself." And he continued to chuckle, lugubriously.

"Well, what do I do?" I asked. "The men are worried. Felix Galimir is the concertmaster, and you know he is a serious, knowledgeable player if there ever was one, and he says the program just can't come off this way."

The critic was one of those people, and I've met others, to be sure, who don't listen, but when you finish talking automatically indicate disagreement. "No, that's not it," was his retort to almost everything I ever said to him. "No, that's not it." And then quite often, he would say almost exactly what I had just said. Very disconcerting.

So he said, "No, that's not it. The old man knows what he's doing. Anyway, what the hell do you want me to do about it?"

"Well, you are a good friend of his, and he should know what the men feel about the rehearsals, I think."

"No, that's not it. He knows what he wants. Relax."

The next day at rehearsal, when Beecham knocked off at the hour-and-a-half mark, still wasting an hour of needed work time, Galimir, the concertmaster, approached him.

"Sir Thomas," he said in his soft, always slightly deferential but completely winning manner, "excuse me, but I think we need more rehearsal. This orchestra, after all, doesn't play together as much as most, and some of the music is difficult. Tomorrow is the last rehearsal. Please don't think me disrespectful, Sir Thomas."

"Not at all, dear boy. Not at all. (That's a nice jacket, by the way. Get it here?) It will be just fine. Just fine. Good lord, where is that damned manager? Has me cigars." I hurried up with his cigars.

The upshot was that the concert went fairly well. The critics of the daily papers gave it very favorable notices; by this late date in his career, Beecham was the kind of institution that was always praised. After all, who would want to risk having panned his last concert? But we got one critical blast. From my friend and sometime employee, the magazine critic. He thought the concert was an unfair representation of the Beecham art. Why? Because the whole thing sounded underrehearsed.

To return to the matter of Bruno Walter. His telephone connection with Mrs. H. having been broken, I wondered what was in store for me. I called Walter in Chicago and was relieved to hear him answer the phone himself—I was in no state for long delays, especially overnight ones.

Walter was very cordial, which was also good. He always called me Tuvim—a much commoner name than Toobin. Almost any name is. I tentatively broached the Wanda Horowitz matter, but Walter wasn't at all tentative.

"I tell you, Mr. Tuvim, this was really something." Walter spoke the quintessential Viennese English—very musical. I happen to love the sound of it, and I always enjoyed my talks with Walter enormously. He was a man of great culture, not as benevolent as he seemed—he could be as nasty and unreasonable as the best of them—but a marvelous conversationalist. (Columbia has made some records of lengthy interviews with Walter, in which he expresses his thoughts on music and art and living, and they are well worth hearing.) But the Walter talking to me from Chicago was very annoyed—not furious, because he treated it as though it were ridiculous rather than sinister.

"I have known Wanda Toscanini—how long? Better I shouldn't say how long. Stupid she always was, but until tonight I did not think crazy. I will not for Arturo Toscanini conduct *Eroica* symphony? What would I not do for my old dear friend Arturo Toscanini? [I never heard Walter refer to the Maestro in any way other than as Arturo Toscanini—both names every time, as though they were one word.] This woman calls me and tells me about a concert with Horowitz, and I accept, and then she calls me later and says it might be better if I only conduct this program, not the one you will give honoring Arturo Toscanini and we play *Eroica* Symphony. What is this woman, crazy, stupid, what? I perform with her husband later, we have not even a date, and she says I shouldn't conduct *Eroica* Symphony for Arturo Toscanini. What do you think, Mr. Tuvim?"

I thought only one thing—Fritz Reiner.

I called Mrs. H. back and said it was all straightened out with Bruno Walter. I didn't quote his commendation of her sanity and wisdom. I only said that he would conduct *Eroica* Symphony for Arturo Toscanini and where did that leave Fritz Reiner? Now it was Wanda's turn to get nasty. "The hell with him!" she shouted into the phone.

I didn't follow that right away. "The hell with whom?"

"With Reiner. Father always hated him anyway. He played the 'Giovinezza' in Italy long after father's trouble. [This was a reference to the time Toscanini had refused to play the "Giovinezza"—the Fascist hymn—in Italy during the Mussolini regime in the twenties and been slapped in the face by a Black Shirt official for his action. Not long after he left Italy, not to return until after World War II.] I'm glad he won't be conducting. We don't need him."

Distressed as I was to hear that Reiner had lousy politics, I was much more concerned with the delicate, not to say hazardous, operation of disengaging him from the concert.

I called Reiner the next morning. I was hoping that

some servant would answer the phone, for, pusillani-
mous recreant that I was, it was my plan to leave a
message saying that through circumstances beyond my
control, I was disengaging him from the concert, and
that an explanatory letter would follow. I would then get
a team composed of Ernest Hemingway, T. S. Eliot, Ad-
lai Stevenson, and Louis Nizer to write the letter.

But, of course, Reiner himself answered the phone,
and quite literally between gulps, I said, "Dr. Reiner,
there has been some terrible confusion. Bruno Walter is
going to conduct the *Eroica* Symphony at the Toscanini
Concert. You see, he is an old friend of——"

"I see," said Reiner. And, as Mrs. Horowitz would have
put it, the connection was broken. This spared me, for
the moment at least, and I was relieved—for the moment. I knew that I had not yet heard the end of this.

An hour or so later, Walter Prude called, as I kind of
knew he would. He seemed cheerful enough as he
started, in his fine, almost imperceptible Texas accent:
"Hey, Jerry, Reiner just called me. He's going to kill
you." And he tittered, seeming to enjoy the tableau of
Reiner poised over me, a long knife like Dan'l Boone's
in his grip, striking over and over and . . .

I told Prude the whole story, emphasizing heavily the
dominant, nay, exclusive, role of Wanda Toscanini
Horowitz in the rise and fall of Fritz Reiner as conductor of the *Eroica*. Prude listened—at least I assume he
listened—but he made not a sound on the other end of
the wire. When I paused for breath or finished, I don't
remember which, there was again a little laugh, and he
reiterated, "He's going to kill you, old buddy. Stay close
to home for a while, will you, because I'm telling you,
Reiner is going to kill you."

I sat down and wrote Reiner a letter. I told him as much of the real story as I could without having him get in touch with Mrs. H., or adding her to the list of prospective assassinatees. After all, I figured with her dead the Horowitz concert might be cancelled. Otherwise, I had no strong objection to her dispatch. I told Reiner of my admiration for his conducting, of how he had always been the personification to me of the finest in the arts, sciences, and trades; and, in a shameless exhibition of maudlin pseudonostalgia, I evoked my student days at Curtis in Philadelphia, where Reiner was then the head of the conducting department. I told him, in a fine fictive flight, of having stolen into his class, observed his every movement, and memorized his every syllable. It was a wild combination of the passionate and the obsequious; after all, it was addressed to a Hungarian. I read the letter to Prude.

"Nice piece of prose, old buddy. Is any of it true?"

I disdained to answer. I sent the letter and in about a week asked Prude to check with Reiner to see if he had gotten it. "Yes, he got it."

"What did he say?" I palpitated, envisioning a glorious reconciliation.

"Oh he is going to kill you, there's no doubt about it."

Now preparations began for the three-conductor concert and, happily, all went well. Walter was in New York to conduct the Metropolitan Opera; Monteux, who was living in New York, was in town between guest appearances; and Munch came down from Boston for the two rehearsals he requested. We obtained first-class personnel to augment the regular players, our personnel continuing to fluctuate as the economic pressures on individuals made it harder and harder to field a strong group. But this concert was not hard to staff, especially since the word had gotten around about the proposed Horowitz concert and the recording and all the other lagniappes that were thought to be forthcoming, the rumor mills of the music business grinding more fiercely than any other, save perhaps the military. The eventual aggrandizement of the players was reported to be fantastic. The stories naturally had very little to do with the realities of the situation. At any rate, it was potentially lucrative enough to attract some of the best free-lance players in New York, which has the greatest pool of such musicians anywhere in the world.

Walter and I had some talks about both the three-conductor and the Horowitz concerts, and I was grateful for the time with this delightful and wise old musician. He had a startling memory for things that had happened to him in his half century of conducting. Once this almost total recall threw a scare into me, and lost the engagement for one of the players.

Walter looked at me from over his glasses one morning, more than ever like some benevolent old foxy grandpa—Middle-European version—and asked, "Tell me, Mr. Tuvim, Arpad Beluga [not the man's real name], he still plays with you?"

Now Beluga was a fine wind player, but his deportment left something to be desired. With no threat of firing hanging over him, the orchestra operating as it did on a single-engagement basis, he went his merry way harassing conductors and colleagues alike, showing deference only where conductors who recorded with us were concerned. (I must emphasize that recording was the only branch of the business that was remunerative, TV being at that time, as it is still, a rare treat.) So when Walter, sounding friendly, inquired after Beluga, I was pleasantly surprised, anticipating a good word for the bad boy of the group.

"Yes, Dr. Walter," I happily informed him, "Beluga will be your First."

Then Walter really surprised me. "Then I don't conduct. He is a bad man, a bad man. I had trouble with him at the Philharmonic twenty years ago and I am told by my friends he has gotten much worse. So, Mr. Tuvim, either Beluga or me. It is simple."

What a memory. Although there *was* something truly memorable about Arpad Beluga. One conductor, who didn't want to hire Beluga for a TV show, said, when I remonstrated with him about what a fine player he was, "Sure he can play, but what the hell am I supposed to do, hire a keeper for the three days? You leave that guy loose for three days and he'll set fire to the studio." That was Beluga.

I approached the redoubtable one and told him what Walter had said. I expected a hassle and was armed with all kinds of past examples of his derelictions, when *he* surprised me. They were all surprising me those days. "Yeah," he remembered happily across the span of two decades, "I gave him a real hard time. He wanted me to come to his room ten minutes before the concert to talk about the part because I was substituting for the First that night. He got hit by a car. [A happy smile] So I told the personnel manager to tell Walter to go screw himself. There's nothing in the union rules about coaching sessions. If they wanted to pay me, O.K. The personnel manager said they couldn't pay me, so I told him to tell Walter to go screw himself. I knew the part; what the hell could Walter tell me in ten minutes!"

Beluga told the story with relish, savoring the sweetness of his rectitude over the long years. More important, he said he would step out of the Walter concerts. He left, still grinning over his ancient coup. He even came back for one last remembrance. "Christ, was Walter mad! He conducted the whole concert steaming at me. Every time he gave me a cue with the baton it was like he was dueling me and he hoped it was a sword he could slice me up with. It was great." Such, such were the joys of Beluga's youth.

Monteux, when I visited at his apartment near the old Met, talked in Gallic accents of Toscanini. "They said Toscanini had no repertoire. No repertoire. He knew every oh-pehy-ra. Every one. Every note of every one. Mon Dieux, what that man had in his head!"

I talked to him about doing some concerts with us in the future, though it was strictly dream stuff—I hadn't the slightest idea how I would finance a straight concert with Monteux, who was a tough man with a fee. But I said, "Maitre, next year we must do some concerts."

With no hesitation, and a big smile under his great walrus mustache, he answered, "Next year I will be dead." He wasn't. He was to conduct to the very end, in 1964, when he was just short of ninety. At eighty-six he was made principal conductor of the London Symphony.

I also talked to Mrs. Monteux, a jolly round little lady who on my every visit asked if I had ever contemplated converting to Catholicism, talking about it amiably as though it were some minor palliative: a week in the Caribbean or a salt-free diet. She would say, "Oh you ought to go see Bishop Sheen; he is a lovely man. You'll like being Catholic. It is very nice." And at every little table around the room, and there were quite a few, was a neat pile of tracts. Mrs. Monteux always gave me a few as I left, again very lightly pressuring me with words like, "Read these little books. You'll like them and you'll want to be Catholic. It's very nice." She was the sister-in-law of Meyer Davis, the famous society bandleader. She would kid about how Monteux would have been really well off if he had conducted for "coming-out" parties and cotillions rather than the infamous world *première* of Stravinsky's *Le Sacre du printemps,* and the ballets with Nijinsky, and other historic events.

I asked Monteux only once about the *Sacre première,* with the attendant riot that was the great *scandale* of modern music history, because I figured he was good and sick of talking about it after all these years. He laughed and said, "Oh yes, Le Massacre du printemps" (an old musical chestnut in Paris, I was later told, but new to me). That is all he said, and I didn't bring it up again. When I complained to him about the floating personnel which plagued the Symphony of the Air, he was sympathetic and told me Parisian orchestras had the same problem. Parisian orchestras come and go, their economic problems are apparently also monstrous, and Monteux told me about one he worked with.

They were performing *Harold in Italy* by Berlioz, which calls for a viola soloist. There were to be three rehearsals and the concert. After the first two rehearsals, a substitute violist appeared for the third, saying that his predecessor was indisposed (the standard dodge), and since the first violist had been pretty bad, Monteux wasn't overcome with grief. The rehearsal proceeded, and to the Maitre's delight the violist was marvelous. They finished, and Monteux was very happy and praised the soloist lavishly. The violist thanked Monteux, and added, "Oh, and the player you will have at the concert is even better than I am."

The Munch rehearsals went smoothly, and became memorable for one delightfully raucous visit from members of the Barrault-Renaud troupe, which was playing New York then. Munch had not seen many of these people for years, and there was an emotional reunion, with that wonderful chattering that accompanies such French tableaux. My ignorance, however, threw a minor pall on the proceedings. I was quite overwhelmed to have M. Barrault himself approach me and ask if the music director of the troupe could have a ticket for the three-conductor concert. I said, "Of course," breaking my resolve not to give out any complimentaries; but M. Barrault is a supreme charmer. He called the music director, a short swarthy fellow, and when I asked his name so that I could leave his ticket, he spoke very softly, and I couldn't make it out. It sounded like Boonyez or Booryez. I said, "I'm sorry. Could you spell it please?"

He looked very annoyed, and practically spat out the letters. "Boulez. B-o-u-l-e-z." It was Pierre Boulez, already an important figure in the modern music world, and he certainly made it clear to me that he was not amused by my lack of recognition.

The three-conductor concert was an artistic success, the reviews excellent, but none of the great hopes for financial miracles materialized. As is inevitable in the orchestra business, costs—orchestra salaries, house rental, stage hands, and so forth, and so forth—just about consumed the box-office take, even at the higher prices charged. We scaled the house from five to fifteen dollars. The profit was under five thousand dollars. Thus you can imagine the net on a regularly priced concert. None of the fringe benefits ensued because again costs would have ruined the chance for any recording or broadcast entrepreneurs to make money. When I made appeals about the historic importance of the concert, I was greeted with either stony or amused looks. "You can't eat history," said one tycoon with a knack for turning a phrase.

But there was still the Horowitz concert to come, and that couldn't miss. Could it?

Since the program was built around the B Flat Concerto, we decided to make it all Brahms. Walter called me to come over and complete the program, and when I arrived he was happy, saying, "Ah, we have a fine program. With the concerto we will play the *Tragische Ouvertüre* and the Haydn Variations. It is given, no?" I imagine he meant the program was self-evident or preordained, but whether by God or by the timing involved I wasn't sure. Certainly it was a fine list. And then he asked, "What have we decided on for a date?" I said the first possible date available in Carnegie was May 10, and anyway Horowitz had been insistent that he have until that date to prepare.

"Oh," ohed Walter, "not until May. [It was now, remember, the middle of February.] You know, Mr. Tuvim, I think we should do it in the fall."

That sentence will live with me forever. Fall. That was the word. That was the concept. That was the result. Fall. Fall. I knew very well that it was highly problematical whether Horowitz would ever play that concert whenever it took place. He was not at all well at this time. Emil Gilels had visited him when he was in New

York and told me, "Horowitz very seeck. Very very seeck. Will not play for long time." And everything I heard from the Horowitz domicile corroborated Gilels. Mrs. Horowitz's proposal of the concert was a stunner chiefly because of these numerous alarming reports about Horowitz's condition. I was certain that any long-range postponement would doom the project. I had to be extremely careful with Walter because he had made it clear from the first that he was every bit as important to the concert as Horowitz. To him it was another concert, another way to honor Arturo Toscanini. To me it was a really huge box office, just as a start.

Here is an indication. The Sunday after I had made the arrangements with Mrs. Horowitz, Miles Kastendieck, in the then extant *World-Telegram,* made a one-sentence statement at the end of his music column. It read: "Rumor has it that Vladimir Horowitz will come out of retirement this spring to play a memorial concert for Arturo Toscanini with the Symphony of the Air and Bruno Walter." That is all it said. The next morning, and for the next three days, our telephone facilities were absolutely swamped with requests for information. Our meagre little staff pleaded with me to have a recorded announcement made because they were frantic. I decided against it because it was expensive (by our lights) and because I was afraid our creditors, seeing instant wealth just over the horizon for us, would move against us in advance. I also didn't think it very seemly for our friends at the Internal Revenue Service not to get at least their weekly chance to harass and threaten us. Admittedly, they were getting nothing else. Even more amazing than the phone calls were the letters, huge piles of them, many with checks for amounts of from ten to two hundred dollars, saying things such as, "Send me two tickets for any date, any location." One even had the touching sentiment "keep the change" affixed.

The fringe benefits for the Horowitz concert were not illusory. A contract existed for a recording of the concerto, and there was also to be an album of the whole concert. The TV folks, still crying poverty, were really talking business though, this time, and there was even a publisher who wanted to do a picture book on the program. This may have been just another concert to Walter; to me it had a priority just below oxygen. In fact, I felt, if this one gets away, the hell with the oxygen. So I began to try to impress Walter with the urgencies of this concert for the men of the orchestra and for the whole future of the Symphony. And I was accurate and truthful. I was even tempted to promise the execution of Beluga if that would help.

Walter immediately made the situation clear—and I was surrounded, and soon to be destroyed. "I'm sorry, Mr. Tuvim, but you see Columbia wants to record Bruckner Seventh and Ninth Symphony with me in California, and I want to do it in May. I must be there by the first of May. We can work something out for the fall. Don't worry." (This to a dying man.) I tried. I told him Columbia would probably postpone the sessions. After all their President Goddard Lieberson was one of the fathers of the whole idea, and he was indeed being very helpful to me in attempting to set up a television program and had also helped with the recording contract. In fact I know that Lieberson told Walter the sessions could be postponed for any time the conductor wanted. But Walter was adamant. Apparently "it was given" that the Bruckner be recorded early in May. And

I was trapped by the inexorable fact that the excitement over Horowitz was annoying to Walter, and he seemed to be looking for a way to manifest his own indispensability.

When I told Mrs. Horowitz of these developments and timorously suggested that we think about another conductor, she demurred. After all, I suspected there was a certain amount of relief involved, for Mrs. H. could not help but think of the Herculean task of getting Volodye ready for that concert. I could even, when it looked promising, remember picturing her certain travail in getting him to rehearsal, and then on that fateful May day, getting him to Carnegie. Perhaps it is a sad rationalization, but there is a good chance that, Walter or not, there would never have been a Horowitz concert. Anyway, the envelopes with the checks were returned, the recording was cancelled, and the TV people were free to go back to their "I Love Lucy," and the rental of Carnegie Hall was revoked. The tributes by the Symphony of the Air to Arturo Toscanini were over, except those in the hearts and minds of his men, which will go on forever.

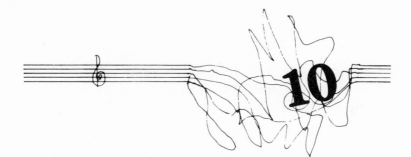

Now it is the winter of 1973; yet the alarums and excursions of the more than eight years that ended in the spring of 1963 still sound very near as I remember those days which look long ago when you look at one of those calendars that Stoki despised, but which are vivid enough to me to make me still play the game over in my mind constantly. If I had only done this; if I had only not done that. If I had been more politic; if I had cared less about the programs and more about cultivating the monied. And as I write these sentiments, I feel the uselessness of hindsight and the impotence of my position. Certainly I made mistakes and miscalculations. There was a basic flaw: once NBC scuttled the orchestra, no one and nothing could really have salvaged it. And it went on too long, the salvaging effort, that is. Ego played too big a part—the refusal, perverse I'm afraid, to admit that I was defeated. That circumstances (almost always spelled *money*) made it unseemly to continue past a certain point. The music critic, he of the snarling cynicism, Beecham's loathsome friend, did say it well in one of his conversations with me.

"You've got to realize, Toobin, that this orchestra was once Tiffany's. And half the time it's now Woolworth's."

Well, if we had had underwriting or subsidy or massive luck, there were enough fine musicians in New York, both from the Toscanini era and after, to make it —well, I don't know about Tiffany's. Maybe Korvettes, for a while. And later, with the right conductor and a fixed personnel and a fairly regular season—who knows? But as I write about 1963, I read now of great upheavals on the music scene that make me seem more of a seedy Don Quixote than ever. The Philharmonic strikes for weeks, the ballet orchestra has major difficulties, the deficit at the Metropolitan gets so astronomical that they lose all meaning to the outsider (and to the insider too, I imagine). All the Symphony of the Air episode did was illustrate the callousness of the corporate sponsor, when he felt he had done enough. I think NBC made money on the orchestra; the record sales probably paid for the concerts. I am no savant of this type of complex economics (or any kind), but I find it hard to believe that the hardheads at the Radio Corporation of America would subsidize a losing venture for almost twenty years. Yet, who knows? Perhaps a romantic passion for music, like mine, dwelt in the breast of General Sarnoff. Perhaps Chotzinoff thought sincerely that the best way to honor Maestro Toscanini was to let his last orchestra die with him.

"It is a hard world," impresario Hurok once said to me when I complained at some of the fees he was asking for his artists—Tiffany's all—or almost all. Here was this great dispenser of "culture for the masses" (a phrase he used over and over) assuring me that it was tough—"a hard world." Certainly he didn't make it any easier, and I guess he had to act the way he did, too. Yet a Hurok story sums up for me the business of music, and I tell it for that reason.

Hurok is to my mind the great impresario of our time, maybe of all time. His list has been, and still is, fantastic. The best in music and dance. A Hurok attraction means something. And I think he took chances with his own money: you have to risk capital to bring over the great Soviet ballet companies and so on—as Hurok always reminded his interviewers. Yet when I saw the great man last year, at eighty-five (a short time before his death), striding from his limousine to his office on Sixth Avenue, it appeared to me that somehow the risks had not been too precipitous; the impresario had survived them and was doing very nicely, thank you, in the twilight of his career. But here is an example of how the Great Man treated the Symphony of the Air as it careened down the road to ruin.

We decided to give a series of five concerts in the season of 1961–1962, hoping thus to establish ourselves in Carnegie Hall, which kept talking about a resident orchestra after the Philharmonic moved to Lincoln Center. Hurok's lieutenant, Walter Prude, suggested Alfred Wallenstein, for twenty-five years music director of the Los Angeles Philharmonic, and a musician I had always admired since my days as a student when I heard his fabulous performance of the cello part in the recording of Strauss's *Don Quixote* that Beecham made with the Philharmonic in 1928 or so. The men in the orchestra were less than enthusiastic, Wallenstein having a reputation as a very nasty fellow. (This was, unfortunately, deserved.) Wallenstein was a consummate musician, knew technically the craft of conducting as well as most maestri around. But he was terribly inarticulate and just couldn't convey to the players what he wanted. Some conductors can, and they can do it with words or gestures or just with the baton. Wallenstein, with word or stick or anything else, lacked that magic. And as his frustration over his lack of communication grew, he became abusive and his rehearsals became terrible ordeals. Still, our options were very limited, and besides, being a Hurok artist gave Wally, as he was known in the business, some éclat. Most significant, Hurok had hinted that if we took Wally, who needed building up as a name after eight or nine years of modest activity in the post-Los Angeles period, he would look kindly on our project. I took this to mean that he would scale his usually high fees downward to accommodate the poverty-stricken but aspiring Symphony of the Air.

My first disillusionment came at the initial meeting to arrange for soloists. It was obvious that we would need big names to fill the hall; Wally certainly wasn't going to do it. We decided on a Beethoven cycle. As we went into Hurok's office, I met in the hall an old friend, the pianist Van Cliburn. We had gotten to know each other right after Van came back from the USSR and his great Tchaikovsky Prize triumph. The orchestra had been hired by Columbia Concerts, then Van's managers, for a tour of some five or six cities, and some recording. I liked Van, although his concepts of political reality were what I remembered best. Old Van talked Texas-English, and was not averse to pontificating. "Jayy [that's how Jerry came out in Cliburnese], I told Mister Kroowschef that ah think that if everybody just started lovin' everybody else—raht now—just started lovin' everybody—there wouldn't ever be another war ever. And Mr. Kroowschef said, 'Wahn—you said it.' Ah swear, he said 'Wahn—you said it.'" Anyway, I liked old Van, and

I was genuinely glad to see him outside of Hurok's office.

"What are you doin' here, Jayy?"

"Walter and Wally and I are seeing Mr. Hurok about a series we're giving this season."

I gave a brief description of the series.

"Haay, Jayy, that sounds great. Can I play in it?"

"Sure," I gulped, seeing at least one sold-out house for certain. "Should I ask Mr. Hurok?"

"What are you goin' to ask him for? I remember how nice you and the rest of the boys were to me when I came back from Russia, and I would do anything for you. Just work the date out with Walter."

So in I went to the Great Presence, with one trophy already in the bag. The meeting seemed to bore Hurok. He agreed to let us have Emil Gilels, but asked a fee of $3000. Wally broke in at this point, and sputtered—he always sputtered when he was mad, which was most of the time.

"Jesus Christ, Sol. [Wally was one of the only people I ever heard call Hurok Sol. Certainly Prude never did, and he had been with the company almost twenty-five years. And Wally's favorite expletive was "Jesus Christ." A generation of musicians was inured to hearing Wallenstein sputter, "Jesus Christ, fellahs, do it again, will you?"] *Three thousand.* How in the hell are they going to make any dough paying that kind of fee?" Well said, Wally, sputtering or not. And Prude entered the lists, though deferentially, very clearly.

"Well, really, Mr. Hurok. This series is kind of make-or-break for these fellows. I didn't think we were going to treat this series purely as a commercial venture."

Hurok—always looking like a Buddha in back of his huge, Mussolini-like desk, with the huge autographed pictures as backdrop—peered steadily at Prude, and you could catch behind the thick glasses a glint of malevolence.

"Volter. Let me tell you something. *You're* a commoishel venture. I vunt three thousand for Gilels and dots dot."

We next arranged for the New York debut of Igor Oistrakh, son of David, but no more like his father than I like Hercules.

Then Hurok suggested (and his suggestions had all the uncertainty and tentativeness of a Parris Island drill sergeant's) that we have the then little-known Daniel Barenboim as a soloist in one of the piano concertos. Wallenstein was no admirer of the teenage Barenboim and said so in unequivocal terms, not sparing the "Jesus Christ" one bit.

"J. C., Sol, what the hell do we want that kid for? He doesn't even play too good for a little boy, and I thought we were going to get some good names for this thing."

Hurok, who never answered anything directly that I could ever notice, began to run through how many engagements young Barenboim had for that season, and even unburdened himself of a witticism. "Don't you want Haddasah ticket parties?" Barenboim was an Israeli, and his publicity at that time, such as it was, stressed the fact.

Barenboim—Danny to everyone—had actually made his New York debut with the Symphony of the Air, when he was about fourteen, in a benefit concert for some Jewish organization, as I recall, with Stokowski conducting. He played the Prokofiev First Concerto with great *brio,* although there didn't seem to be much except technical dash in the playing. What I remember best—or worst—about the occasion was what happened after the concerto. Danny got a good, if not overwhelming, ovation, and Stoki, never too happy about soloists intruding on his concerts, began impatiently to ask the music librarian to get ready for the next number. Then, after two curtain calls, to my consternation, Danny seated himself at the piano and started on an encore—a Bach-Busoni. Stoki could never abide encores, except those he himself conducted, and we even had a house rule in Philadelphia—later copied other places—against them. So there I stood, raised as I had been in that Spartan tradition, next to the sire of that tradition, while the brash little Danny ripped through his Bach-Busoni. (It was one of the fast ones.) Stoki just glared, the famous eyebrow went up. The little so-and-so hadn't even had him out for a joint bow before launching into this extra.

Danny finished. The applause started again. Stoki looked right at me. "Tell that boy to go home," he said. And he went into his dressing room.

Danny took one more bow. The applause was moderate, and I guess he could have milked it for one more return. But I went to him, and while I didn't tell him to go home, I did indicate that he should get lost. "Stokowski's mad," I said. "We don't play encores around here."

Danny in those days was very obedient, and he did look upset over my report of Stoki's displeasure, and he did get lost. Barenboim has been extremely successful and, from the few performances that I have heard, seems very gifted as a conductor. For a while after his piano debut, he was in constant touch with me. (In fact, the only Hanukkah card I ever remember getting was from Danny Barenboim.) But as his fame grew, I heard less and less from him, and recently when I bumped into him on Riverside Drive, he was rather cool, asking me what I was doing, without seeming to be listening to the answer, and only becoming animated when I told him I had read in that very morning's *Times* that the czar of conducting managers, Ronald Wilford, was lusting after Danny's contract; the only conductor, Wilford complained, that he wanted and didn't have.

But Wally never cared for Barenboim, and there was a battle royal over whether or not he would appear in our series. I don't remember what happened except that Danny *did* play in the series, and the warmhearted Wally remarked as Danny was taking a bow for the Beethoven C Minor Concerto, "How in the Christ can this kid fool so many people. Phooey!"

I was tempted to mention the Cliburn incident to Hurok, but I refrained. The meeting ended with Hurok still a little put out with Prude over the "commercial-venture" effrontery, and as we were leaving, he said to me, "You stay in touch with Volter; he'll give you plenty of bargains." And he didn't sound too happy at the prospect.

I told Walter about Van's offer, and he said he would talk to him and set a date. Cliburn agreed to appear on the first program and play the *Emperor,* which he did very well. I am a Cliburn enthusiast, and while some of my *aficionado* friends disagree, I think that with Vladimir Ashkenazy he is at the top of the new generation of piano virtuosi.

Cliburn did play at the first concert; I thought he was marvelous; the critics said he was not at home in the classical repertoire (I thought the critics were full of soup, to wax quaint); and about three weeks after the concert I got a phone call from impresario Hurok.

Now I used to get in to see the impresario now and then, and he used to tell people that he liked me and admired my courage in trying to keep the orchestra alive. ("He's a nice boy, but I wish he would get a *real* job. That orchestra of his is going nowhere!") But Hurok and I were not exactly buddies; I was never tapped for luncheon at the table he kept permanently reserved at Le Pavillon, nor was I ever invited to one of the post-ballet openings which he sprung on the St. Regis roof. So I was flabbergasted when I was told that the impresario wanted me on the telephone. And I was hardly prepared for what ensued.

"Hallo, Toobin. [I was kind of flattered that he even knew or remembered my name.] Why haven't you paid Wahn yet for his concert with you?"

I have a very quick mind; I must readily admit it. I have lots of faults and infirmities, but I have a very quick mind. And I saw this thing unreeling very quickly.

"Well, Mr. Hurok. The day you saw me and Wally and Walter about the series, I bumped into Van . . . ," and I told what happened exactly as it happened.

"No such thing. I had lunch with the boy and the mother yesterday at Pavillon. [Why did he have to bring that up, as though to remind me that only the elite got invited there by *him*.] And I asked the boy vy he didn't get yet the fee from you, and he said he didn't know."

Oh my mind works quick, all right. I saw among other hideous visions or previsions the cancellation of the whole series because Hurok was pulling out his artists. All of them were pullable, too, because all of them were from the impresario's stable, even Wally, though I knew he wasn't in exactly the same demand as "Wahn." But I fought back—sort of.

"Look, Mr. Hurok, we were friendly ever since Van got back from Russia. We played all his concerts when he came back for his tour." (Even as I said it, I knew that was lead-balloon material, because Hurok wasn't even managing Cliburn then). "Anyway, Walter—" and here I hesitated. I didn't want to implicate Walter Prude, gentleman and friend. I could still see the thick glinting glasses and Hurok leaning toward the gentleman and friend and the immortal lines, "Volter, you're a commoishel venture." I didn't want Hurok thinking there was much of an alliance between me and Prude. Alliances with me spoke very little for a manager's business acumen.

"Vot about Volter?" Hurok interrupted as I mulled over implicating Prude. "Volter has nothing to do with it. I spoke to the boy and the mother, and they don't know anyting about anyting. I *know* that Wahn gets five thousand dollars a concert and I want him paid."

This was ludicrous. I was certain that we didn't have $5000 in our account; I wasn't even sure we had $500.

"Well, I better talk to Van, Mr. Hurok. There is really some mistake."

"There's no mistake, except maybe you. [I thought that was nasty. I thought people said he liked me.] I vunt the boy paid. I saw the boy and the mother . . ." At this point I tuned out, hearing something vague about lawyers and attachments. I immediately tried to put a call through to Van who was living in a hotel across the street from Carnegie. The switchboard told me he and his mother were gone for about three months—on tour. I should have known that the minute the impresario called. I called Prude, who said nothing, but called back later to say that Hurok would be willing to take half the fee, and to wait a reasonable time for payment. When I tried to discuss the matter with Walter, he said, "What's the use?" I agreed. We paid Hurok $2500 in an unreasonable period of time.

I tell the Hurok story because in its way it typifies the terrible business of music as I found it in the period 1955–1963, during which I tried to make the former NBC Symphony Orchestra the second major orchestra in New York. It was not unique; it is only that Hurok was so well known, indeed about the only at-all-known impresario in history. His only challenger is Diaghilev, I suppose, and that notable figure confined himself entirely to the world of the ballet. I can think of no manager at any level who ever did anything for the orchestra but try to make money from us, and from showcase artists who were having difficulty getting engagements with the standard organizations (the Philharmonic, the Met, and so forth).

In order to keep some cash flow coming in, the orchestra had to take many engagements that were at best routine—accompanying an artist who wanted to do the concerto repertoire, for example, and couldn't get hired by any orchestra in New York—and at worst downright demeaning—a well-to-do dilettante who, tired of conducting his hi-fi set, engaged the symphony for two or three rehearsals and a concert attended chiefly by his family and friends. There were quite a few such grisly events, and they were at times made positively ghastly by the conductor's insistence on playing his or her own compositions. God, what sounds would occasionally emanate from the stage at Carnegie Hall! But the need for funds was so great that all but the rankest musical frauds could obtain the services of an orchestra that still contained over fifty per cent of the men who had played the last seasons of Maestro Toscanini. And there on the Sunday music page of the *Times* was the ad, to my shame and embarrasment: "JOSEPH Q. GLUTZ conducting the SYMPHONY OF THE AIR in a program including works of Beethoven, Wagner and the World Premiere of Glutz's Symphony No. 1 *(Reminiscenses of Teaneck, New Jersey)*. Remaining seats now at the Box Office." And how many seats remained at the box office depended on how big a family Maestro Glutz had.

Two or three days before the concert, with about two thousand five hundred seats remaining, my staff would add to its usual duties of hiding me from bill collectors and arguing with insistent musicians that their last-due checks would be available momentarily the odious task of "papering" a house for a concert that nobody wanted to come to. Don't imagine for a moment that it is easy to give tickets away for a Glutz concert at Carnegie Hall. We would post operatives at subway entrances, the main reading room of the library, music schools for the young, homes for the aged, and even on one storied occasion, the penitentiary at Rikers Island (tickets also being made available for guards, of course). Still, these "vanity" concerts would always play to three-quarters-empty houses, the last two tiers invariably being closed off. The musicians of course would grumble, accuse me of prostitution at the streetwalker level, but scramble for the engagements which paid on the average about sixty-five dollars for the aforesaid rehearsals and concert. And don't think they didn't butter up Glutz and tell him that sections of *Reminiscences of Teaneck* were redolent of Bruckner. (They would later mutter to their deskmates that they were referring to Sam Bruckner of Teaneck, New Jersey.) And the helpful critics, all of them I knew and all of whom, well, most of whom, knew that it was sheer desperation and the hope of a better tomorrow that led me to take such shabby jobs, would write condescending reviews, clucking at the ignominy of it all, and for the umpteenth time decrying the fall of the mighty.

One critic, now at the peak of his profession, had lunch with me on a Tuesday, assured me that I had done everything humanly possible to make the orchestra survive, and even regaled me with tales of my heroism that I didn't remember, but that lifted my flagging spirits. Then on the following Sunday appeared a piece by my admirer (and come to think of it, I paid for the lunch), lamenting the imminent fall of the Symphony of the Air, and noting that while there were good ideas, and noble ambitions, the project was failing for weak management and poor administration. And I dare say he was right. No alibis. I was no miracle worker, that's for sure. And I never really got Sisyphus's rock up the hill. I just believed that New York should have a second major orchestra, that the great aggregation put together for Arturo Toscanini should be preserved, and that in a city and environs that contained over ten million people, I would find a way. For various reasons, some funny, some tragic, some inevitable, some occasioned by my own ineptness, I failed miserably. But I think it was worth the effort.

It may be of some interest to the reader to know what happened to the manager of the Symphony of the Air after the debacle. Putting aside the psychic and physical trauma (which wasn't too easy, but was no worse than that of any man who sees ten years of maniacal effort and daily anxiety end in failure and humiliation), I *was* jobless. As to the humiliation, nothing succeeds like success, and nobody loves a loser. And I felt like the coach or manager of one of those many Philadelphia teams that I had followed through the years as a displaced Philadelphian. For one thing, the manifestations of loserdom began to pile up. The telephone, which used to ring a lot, even in the bad times, even when every ring was ominous and portended trouble and danger, began to fall strangely silent. An amazing number of my contacts and "friends" didn't seem to be agonizing over what was happening to me. To be sure, an occasional creditor, undeterred by the general opinion that the Symphony of the Air was as dead as the proverbial doornail, called, with a half-hearted threat here, a denunciatory attack there.

Rumors circulated among musicians which "considerate" acquaintances made known to me; and musicians, as I've stated previously, ranked with the military as premier rumormongers. My favorite, disseminated by our old friend Arpad Beluga, whom Bruno Walter had revered so much, was to the effect that I had absconded to Mexico with "all the funds" of the Symphony. Since "all the funds" consisted of about fourteen dollars left in the petty-cash box, and I was already being hounded for it, most of those who heard the wind player's charge merely attributed it to his long-rumored dementia. But I, languishing on Eighty-sixth Street near Riverside Drive, and wondering if I would ever again see Asbury Park, let alone Acapulco, saw no humor in it at all. My wife, a sturdy soul, more stable, more sensible than I or any of my "artistic" compeers, told me to get out of the house and find gainful, constructive employment, though she was not at all charmed by the fact that not only had I not absconded with any funds, but I was already under threat from a legion of the unpaid, ranging from printers of programs through renters of timpani to the intrepid minions of the Internal Revenue Service who demanded of me, as the putative leader of the Symphony, all unpaid (and they were very substantial) taxes.

My lawyers pleaded, and are, alas, still pleading that this was a cooperative corporation, as indeed it was, and that the entire membership was equally responsible. Naturally, at this juncture, the forces of the orchestra, officers who had a major role in running the business of the group, and players who had made a considerable amount of money through the years of concerts, both the Glutzy and the good ones, and recordings, which even a cursory inspection of the Schwann catalogues through the years will show were numerous, turned all inquiries and demands on to me. Oh, Beluga, would that I were in Mexico or Samoa or on the not-yet visited Sea of Tranquillity, when you had me sunning myself on the Gulf, my pockets abulge with lucre. It was a hard time, and it was so complicated and messy that it is still not over. Bizet said it for me and so many others who had dreams but lacked the genius or the strength or the luck to make a reality of them in the musical realms of gold.

"Music," commented bitterly the composer of *Carmen,* "what a Glorious Art; what a Hideous Profession." It was for me.

Acknowledgments

Three men, having in common the qualities of a universality of interest, an incredible knowledge of many disciplines, and a feeling, however misguided, that the tales of my journey through the dark wood called the music world should be perpetuated, were the prime movers in my writing this book. They were, and are, friends and inspirations: Angus Cameron, Senior Editor and Vice President of Alfred A. Knopf; Al Silverman, Executive Editor of the Book-of-the-Month Club; and my editor, and so much more, Alan Williams of Viking Press. Struggling through the composition with me, patiently reading sections, and giving invaluable advice from their own creative lives in the arts were Walter Neiman, General Manager of WQXR; Richard Pack, great pioneer and innovator in all that has been best in radio and television for a quarter of a century; and Walter Prude, Vice President of Hurok Concerts, who in his own person exemplifies what the music business can be, and so rarely is.

Merrill Pollack and Cork Smith of Viking bore with me in the early days of my work and were enormously helpful. My colleague and friend Marrie Campbell took time from a hectic existence as chief researcher of "Bill Moyers' Journal" to type the manuscript, and in the process made excellent stylistic and structural suggestions.

My son, Jeffrey (who would rather be called Jeff, but who may forgive his father for the formality in this, his first book), was always urging me to get on with the work, would even deign now and then to read a page or two, and in his cool, worldly, thirteen-year-old manner, would mutter, "Pretty good—I think."

And finally, my wife, Marlene Sanders, a great television producer, who always managed to work harder than I did, still took time to read the manuscript, and to make an infinity of discerning judgments as to what I should leave in and what I should take out. All this, even though in sixteen years of marriage she has had to hear all the stories in this book over and over and over— whenever I would find a willing or unwilling ear. No greater love hath any woman. And no greater woman hath any man.